Equipped to Enjoy

LIFE'S JOURNEY

SURPORA SPARKS-THOMAS

Copyright © 2014 by Surpora Sparks-Thomas

Equipped to Enjoy Life's Journey
by Surpora Sparks-Thomas

Printed in the United States of America

ISBN 9781498410304

All rights reserved solely by the author. The author guarantees all contents are original and do not infringe upon the legal rights of any other person or work. No part of this book may be reproduced in any form without the permission of the author. The views expressed in this book are not necessarily those of the publisher.

Scripture quotations taken from the King James Version (KJV) – public domain

Scripture quotations taken from the Amplified Bible (AMP). Copyright © 1954, 1958, 1962, 1964, 1965, 1987 by The Lockman Foundation. Used by permission. All rights reserved.

Scripture quotations taken from The Message (MSG). Copyright © 1993, 1994, 1995, 1996, 2000, 2001, 2002. Used by permission of NavPress Publishing Group. Used by permission. All rights reserved.

Scripture quotations taken from the New International Version (NIV). Copyright © 1973, 1978, 1984, 2011 by Biblica, Inc.™. Used by permission. All rights reserved.

Scripture quotations taken from the The Living Bible (TLB). Copyright © 1971 by Tyndale House. Used by permission. All rights reserved.

Scripture quotations taken from the New American Standard Bible (NASB). Copyright © 1960, 1962, 1963, 1968, 1971, 1972, 1973, 1975, 1977, 1995 by The Lockman Foundation. Used by permission. All rights reserved.

Front Cover Photo is by: Zipporah Leah Wilson

www.xulonpress.com

Table of Contents

Dedication vii
Acknowledgement ix
Forward xi
Preface xiii

Chapter 1 Getting Ready for the Journey 19
    Introduction
    The Mode of Transportation
    Comparison of the Body to a Car

Chapter 2 Factors Influencing Decisions 29

Chapter 3 Impregnated With God's Word 35
    Factors that Promote an Enjoyable Journey

Chapter 4 Spiritual Growth Resources 39
    Decreeing What You Believe
    Live by Faith
    Activating Spiritual Laws
    Prerequisite Questions for Spiritual Growth Level

Chapter 5 Levels and Characteristics of Spiritual Growth 47
    Seasons of Life

Chapter 6 A Three-Step Return on Investment (ROI) Process . . 57
    Sacrifice/Counting the Cost

Return on Investment
Attributes of Faith

Chapter 7   Unexpected Roadblocks 65
Self-imposed Roadblocks
God's Word Is Health
Laughter and Joy as best Remedies for Stress

Chapter 8   Preparation for the Unexpected 71

Chapter 9   Confirming the Plans through Praise and Worship ... 75

Chapter 10   Is Your Transportation Reliable? 81
How Often to Stop for Fuel
Benefits from Reading and Meditating God's Word
Maintenance Check-Up
Check Oil and Lubricant—Love Walk

Chapter 11   Reasons People Err 91
The Remedy when Error Occurs
Being Transformed by the Renewing of Your Mind
Successful Arrival at Our Destination
Bibliography

About the Author 99
Summary 101

Dedication

This book is dedicated to the Glory of God for His faithfulness and commitment to keeping all of His Promises. I honor Jesus Christ for salvation and all that He has done, continue to do and will do. I praise Him for calling, anointing and entrusting me to teach revelation knowledge of His Word that He imparts to me by the Holy Spirit communicating with my spirit.

I also dedicate this book to the memory of my parents Mr. & Mrs. Charles C. Sparks, Sr. They taught me, and my seven siblings many life lessons. Those lessons continue to influence our decision making and inspire us to do our best. They introduced us to Jesus Christ, lived His principles and taught us to develop a close personal relationship with Him. It is because of my parents that I know how to recognize and view all problems as opportunities to create success stories under the direction of The Holy Spirit.

My mother during her lifetime would visit book stores with me and often ask "When am I going to see your book on one of these shelves?" Before I could respond, she would then say, "You need to document and publish the revelation knowledge that Christ is giving you". I didn't do that before her transition into heaven so I honor her memory with this book.

This book is also dedicated to my family. To my husband, children and their spouses, grandchildren and great grandchild for their faith, unfailing love and support.

Lastly, this book is dedicated to all the readers who will be blessed by reading and timely applying what they learn. Prayerfully, they will engage in activities that will consistently encourage and empower them to live the joyous life that they are equipped to do.

Acknowledgments

I could not have written this book without direction of The Holy Spirit and the great team of multi-gifted and talented people that assisted me in the journey. My daughter, Julena Gayle Johnson encouraged me to write this book and supported me until the manuscript was submitted to the publishing company. We researched various publishing companies, including phone inquires and a telephone interview with me and a representative of Xulon Press. The outcome was that Xulon Press was chosen which has resulted in working relationships with various company representatives.

My youngest daughter Zipporah Leah Wilson provided her artistic and creative abilities to design the front book cover. Leah accepted the invitation during her pregnancy. She reviewed her options during her post partum recovery period after her daughter Taylor was born. She decided to use an original picture of a beautiful sunset that she took while vacationing in Phoenix Arizona. The results of her talent can be seen beautifully displayed on the front cover of this publication.

I was blessed by Mary Agnes (Aggie) Hanks' contributions and many computer skills. Aggie was my Administrative Assistant for 20 years when I was Chief Nurse Executive. I was very pleased when she was able to assist me. Her advanced technical skills were instrumental in getting the manuscript formatted and finalized for submission.

My husband Jule was very understanding and supportive of the time that I had to commit to completing a quality product. As usual, he was a great motivator and cheerleader. With unceasing patience and understanding, He gave me time, space and dedication to complete the manuscript.

My other two daughters, Sonya Faye Thomas, and Sherri Lynn Thomas were great supporters by inquiring and encouraging me to keep my deadlines. They helped me get back on tract whenever unscheduled interruptions or unexpected emergencies occurred.

I am very thankful to all of them for their unselfishness in demonstrating their love, attention and multi-talents to completing the manuscript. I am so blessed and am grateful to God for them.

Foreword

As a human resources training professional, motivational speaker and pastor, I have found that almost everyone is looking for practical solutions to the everyday issues of life. Whether it is for personal life challenges or how to move forward in your career and business, we all desire answers on how to achieve success.

In Equipped to Enjoy Life's Journey, Surpora Sparks-Thomas provides practical advice on how to achieve true success. With her unique style of writing, Surpora has put together a book that will serve as a powerful resource to inspire many to take action and live the kind of full, abundant life that God has promised. With the included self-assessment tool, Surpora ensures that readers will embark upon a journey of self-awareness and spiritual growth as the lessons that she shares are based on scriptural principles found in the Word of God.

I have had the privilege of working with Surpora professionally in the past and have known her for more than a decade. I must say that I have marveled at her ability to live her faith in the professional arena and obtain the ultimate level of respect of her peers because of the content of her character. Because of the level of excellence at which she operates, she was elevated to the Sr. Executive Level of the organization, and numerous awards of recognitions have been bestowed upon her.

As I write this foreword, I am well aware of the fact that Surpora can validate the message of this book by the results that she has achieved in her own life. She has a great family; she serves as a

Certified Christian Life Coach, radio bible teacher, mentor, anointed bible teacher, Director of Christian Education at her church, motivational speaker and Chief Nurse Executive Emeritus of Children's Hospital of Alabama. Surpora is truly equipped and is enjoying her life's journey, and now she wants to share the lessons that she has learned with you. The principles that she outlines in this book will work in a wide range of situations from strategic planning, organizational development, team building, coaching, to routine daily living. As you read this book, you will be inspired to enjoy and live your best life now by optimizing your God-given potential.

William B. O'Neal, Sr.
Pastor, Living Word Church Ministries, Inc.
Inspirational Speaker/Trainer, O'Neal Training & Development, LLC
Sr. Training Consultant, Emory University

Preface

My philosophy of life, love for people and guidance of the Holy Spirit inspired me to write this inspirational, informative and interesting book. The information is timely, truthful, real and relatable. I sincerely believe and have observed in my personal and professional life that all people want to enjoy a prosperous and successful life; but, don't always know how.

My purpose for writing this book is to engage, educate and empower the readers to apply the resulting acquired knowledge and enjoy their life's journey. By reading this book you will appreciate your uniqueness, and your life will be enriched mentally, materially, emotionally and spiritually. You will come to understand that change requires an appropriate intervention. You will get excited in learning and applying interventions in a timely manner to implement and rejoice in the desired change. You will be informed and encouraged by the Scriptures in becoming proficient in living your potential and purpose according to God's Will for your life. It is fascinating to me and a passion of mine to invest in people by mentoring and coaching them to optimize their God-given potential and individuality. It is refreshing to know that God did not make any clones. Each of us should appreciate being in our own skin equipped for peace, productivity, joy and prosperity as God created us.

As we appreciate being in our own skin and develop physically, emotionally, mentally and spiritually we grow in our understanding that life is truly a journey that we should enjoy. Susan E. Wyse,

Marketing Manager, U.S, on February 3, 2012, posted the online Snap qualitative survey poll results for that New Year's Resolutions. According to those results, the most popular, top two (tied) results were lose weight or exercise more and enjoy life more. Trailing a close third was to get organized. The University Of Scranton Journal Of Clinical Psychology posted research results dated January 1, 2014. Enjoying life to the fullest was listed as number four of the top ten 2014 New Years' Resolutions.

The greatest challenge to enjoying your life is to be uncertain of your destiny and you empowering others to define it for you. This empowerment occurs when you agree with the opinions of others about who you are, what you have, what you can become, where you are going, and what you can do. You valuing the opinions of others more than the one you have of yourself can result in performing below your God-given potential. This also sets you up to be deceived, disappointed, discouraged and defeated. Hosea 4:6 says that God's people are destroyed for a lack of knowledge or failure to apply knowledge. So ignorance and intimidation can lead to failure, lack of effectiveness and unhappiness. Reading this book will build your confidence in always referencing and applying the principles in the manufacturer's manual (the Bible) about how we are designed and equipped to succeed. Then your opinion and declarations about your life will be based on the potential and purpose the manufacturer (God) designed in you.

Prosperity and success with joy will not occur if there is a lack of faith, intimidation, lack or failure to appropriately and timely apply relevant information in an effective and efficient way. During my experience as a seasoned executive in the corporate world, I quickly learned that knowledge, zeal and desire do not always guarantee success. I also observed that other's opinion of you and what you can accomplish do not define or influence your destiny unless you allow it. However, the principles and practice of God's Word always results in achievement of defined goals, innovative ideas and unquestionable Godly wisdom. God's instructions to Joshua in Joshua 1:8, informs us that we make our own way prosperous and successful by meditating on God's Word.

Preface

God's Word informs us that life is a gift and journey that should be long, enjoyable, prosperous, and productive. With God, nothing is impossible. His goal for man-kind has always been a "Garden of Eden" lifestyle influenced by our obedience and a close personal relationship with Him through Jesus Christ. God's desire is that our lives affirm that we are equipped and designed to live in authority and victory in His image and His likeness. We are designed to get results just like God and to use His faith and love that was given to us when we accepted Jesus Christ as Lord and Savior. God's way of getting His desired results from Genesis to Revelation is to always speak His desires, expect the outcome, see what He has spoken and expected; and then evaluate it by calling it good. Likewise, we should always speak and pray our desires and not the problem. We should receive our expected results in the spirit by faith by praising and thanking God in Jesus' name before they are manifested in the physical. We know that we have received it when we stop asking. However we must consistently hear, meditate, rightly divide and obey God's Word and the leading of the Holy Spirit to live in victory and take dominion as we are expected to do. Rightly dividing the Scriptures involves knowing the character of the source of the information, the content (what's being said), the context (the framework or background), the culture (way of life) and the confidence that the information is accurate and applicable.

Do you sometimes find yourself unable to take dominion over circumstances as God commanded us?

Is it difficult and challenging for you to always embrace and enjoy your life in all settings and in the presence of all types of personalities?

Do you desire to know how to discover, develop and demonstrate your purpose and value?

Do you want to consistently distribute and deposit in the earth the gifts, talents and other resources that God entrusts you with to be a blessing to others?

Are you clueless about how to create, control and change the circumstances in your environment?

Would you like to learn how to access resources out of the Kingdom of God and live in the supernatural?

If you answered yes to any of these questions, this book is a must read for you. You will learn living biblical principles that you can skillfully apply immediately and be blessed exponentially.

Other questions asked and answered in this book include:

How are you traveling to your eternal destination? Are you stuck in a rut, parked in the past or pressing forward? As you go about your day to day activities, do you stop to think about those simple things, such as which direction are you going today or what are you expecting to happen today?

Information in this book is based on Scriptures, published research, observations, and my professional and personal experiences. The experiences of others are also included. Their information was shared through interviews, networks and published books. There are many who desire a prosperous, victorious and successful life, but don't always know how to joyfully pursue and accomplish it. Reading this book will increase your comfort and competency in developing, planning, achieving and maintaining a joyous life. It can be read independently or studied with a group. It will be best to read it from cover to cover independently first. Afterwards, it will be good for discussion in a book club, bible study class or other forum. After the initial cover to cover read, different subject matters of interest can be studied from the appropriate relevant chapters.

If you have decided, or seeking a way to enjoy your life to the fullest; then reading this book will prove to be an investment with great and valuable returns for you. You will learn how to correctly set and have confidence in your spiritual GPS. You will always know if you are traveling on the straight, narrow and correct route to your destination. You will also detect distractions or any experience that try to cause you to get off course. If you should inadvertently get off the path you will know how to quickly get back on or choose an alternate course as directed by the Holy Spirit. You will then view distractions as an attempt from Satan to deter you from achieving God's perfect plan for your life. So, instead of focusing on the distraction, you will focus on your spirit communicating with the Holy Spirit to lead you around or over road blocks, dead ends, pot holes, and barriers. As with any journey, you must have a plan. I pray that you discover that this book will not only cause you to think about your journey, but inspire you to make timely application of the principles that are outlined within. After all, a journey is simply traveling from one place or destination to another. As you travel from one season of life to another discover, develop and demonstrate different ways to enjoy your life (regardless of the outlook or circumstances). The journey will be worth it. Come travel with me through each chapter of Equipped to Enjoy Life's Journey

Surpora Sparks-Thomas

Chapter 1
Getting Ready for the Journey

Introduction

Have you ever thought about life as an adventurous journey? As you go about your day-to-day activities, do you stop to think about those simple things, such as "Which direction am I going today" or "What am I expecting to happen today?" Because our routines are so defined, we rarely think about the obvious things. That's because we pretty much are following a set pattern, but who set this pattern? Who determined what you would or would not be doing today? We probably haven't thought about it in such a way, but life is like a journey with arrival and departure dates. As with any journey, decisions have to be made. For instance, when you decide to take a trip, there are certain factors to consider. You will first need to decide on the destination, where you are planning to go. Are you going alone or will you take others with you? What route will you take? What mode of transportation will you use? How much fun are you expecting to have on your way and when you arrive? Is there a possibility you will extend your stay if you're having a good time?

Have you ever stopped to think that these are the same decisions or ideas that we will have to make as we prepare to enjoy our journey through life? Everyone has a purpose and a goal, but we get so caught up in the big picture that we sometimes forget that it's the little things that really matter. Regardless of where you are planning to go as you travel life's journey, preparation is required. Preparation is taking place, whether you realize it or not. To be prepared so that you will have a safe and enjoyable journey requires a plan that includes your mode of transportation, travel partner, final destination, the route, costs, weather, and how to deal with unforeseen emergencies. If you fail to prepare, you run the risk of becoming a victim of your circumstances, exposed and susceptible to decisions that others make for you, which may or may not be in your best interest. The same is true as you travel through life. To enjoy your journey, make the decision to plan how to live the best possible life according to the knowledge, experiences, gifts, and talents with which God has blessed you. Learn how to access, activate, and receive the resources that are available in the Kingdom of God for you. Get excited about optimizing each opportunity to "have and enjoy life, and have it in abundance (to the full, till it overflows)" (John 10:10 AMP).

Refuse to empower anyone or anything to determine what kind of day you will have or what you can accomplish. This empowerment occurs when you allow other people or life experiences to create thoughts in you and speak words over you that are not in agreement with God's Word and Will for you. Set the direction of your day with the first words that you speak when you awaken each morning before getting out of bed. Personalize Psalms 118:24 by decreeing that "This *is* the day *which* the Lord hath made; I will rejoice and be glad in it" (KJV). With this confession you are setting your expectations for that specific day without the influences of other people, circumstances, or experiences.

As you reflect on where you are today, take a praise break and ask, "How did I get here? Is this where I want to be today? Did I plan to be here or somewhere else?" Acknowledge that choices you made yesterday or before brought you to this point today. What factors influenced those choices? Was the Holy Spirit included in the planning process? If you planned this as directed by the Holy Spirit and everything went according to plan then you can be excited and grateful that you arrived safely. Now that you are here, is it all that you expected it to be? If not, why not? If so, what are the factors that contributed to your safe and successful arrival? Why did you choose this destination, and where do you go from here? Did your relationships influence or determine your final decision that led you to this destination? Nothing in life just happens; but is a result of someone's previous decisions and/or decrees. Every decision has a predefined consequence and/or reward beyond our control.

Relating life as a journey filled with relationships, romance, risk-taking, responsibility, purpose, promise, promotions, protection, perseverance, and enjoyment is similar to determining, discovering, and developing plans to demonstrate your destiny. So, as you are blessed with information shared in this book, think about the metaphor of envisioning your physical body as transportation for your spirit (which is the real you) to contact and interact with this three-dimensional world that we live in. None of us will live forever in the flesh; but our spirits never die and will live in one of two places after their transition from this world. After Adam and Eve sinned, God decreed that the body was created to last at least 120 years (Genesis 6:3). God desires and has filled the Bible with information on how to live long and strong. After the Israelites' wilderness journey, prior to entering the Promised Land, Moses said in Psalms 90:10 that long life was seventy or eighty years. Moses was referring to all those who did not trust God to do what He had promised. They were the people whose words were contrary to what God decreed in Genesis. They were comparing themselves to the circumstances of the environment that they were going to live in instead of comparing God to the giants that He was going to defeat through them. Their grasshopper image of themselves caused them to die without receiving the blessings that were awaiting them in the Land that God had promised. Is the image that you have of yourself the same as the one that God has of you? It's important to study the Bible to know God's image of you. Know this, that you will only rise and live to the level of the image that you have of yourself. So make the commitment to learn and live up to the image that God has of you. Focus on God as the Problem Solver with all sufficiency and power instead of comparing your insufficiency and inability to your problems. God's unmerited favor and enabling power is always sufficient. Learning and applying the principles in this book will bless you exceeding abundantly above and beyond your current lifestyle. You will be inspired to live out the potential that God designed and engineered inside of you.

The Mode of Transportation

We have been created in God's image and His likeness with the capabilities to think like, act like, speak like, and get the desired results foreordained by Him (Genesis 1:26-28). God's mission, vision, and image of as well as His purposes for man are revealed in Genesis 1:26. As God's Words are spoken in belief by a believer the results are: (1) angels who are strong and mighty are deployed and dispatched as ministering spirits for the believer. They will make sure that the resources are available and accessible to the expectant believer who dispatched them by speaking God's Word; (2) the Holy Spirit as Jesus' representative to us in the earth overshadows while directing God's spoken and believed Word toward the goal. After the goal is reached the Holy Spirit releases the power in God's spoken Word that was put into it by God the Father when He first spoke it; (3) Jesus Christ sitting at the right hand of God represents us as our legal power of attorney in Heaven. He knows the power and value of God's Word as infallible proof that God's Word is not void of power at any time or any situation. Jesus Christ has also confirmed God's Word and has given us the power to create, control, and change any and all circumstances as we speak God's Word in faith; and (4) God, the Father rejoices and is glorified as His Word never returns to Him void.

According to Isa 55:10-11

> [10]For as the rain and snow come down from the heavens, and return not there again, but water the earth and make it bring forth and sprout, that it may give seed to the sower and bread to the eater,[A]
>
> [11]So shall my Word be that goes forth out of my mouth: it shall not return to Me void [without producing any effect, useless], but it shall accomplish

that which I please and purpose, and it shall prosper in the thing for which I sent it (AMP)

According to these Scriptures sometimes the results of speaking, believing, and confessing God's Word will yield immediate results, and at other times patience must have her perfect work, being entire and wanting nothing. The rain immediately waters the ground upon contact with the earth. The snow must melt first; then it waters. In order for snow to melt, sometimes heat from the sun is welcomed and necessary. Rain and snow returns to heaven as mist, indicating their purpose for coming to earth has been served and emptied into the earth. As you remember this, you will not be discouraged or disappointed if you don't experience the desired expected results to your prayers according to your predetermined time frame.

Hold on to your confidence in knowing that God always answers prayer and keeps His Promises (Word). So, return His Word back to Him in prayer and decree that same Word of God to the circumstances that are challenging you. Do both in the mighty and matchless name of Jesus Christ, whose name is above and more powerful than the circumstances that you are experiencing. The circumstances that you speak to have a name and must bow their knees and surrender to the name of Jesus.

Everything that God speaks and does has creative powers and purpose. This includes the birth (transition into the earth) of all people. Everyone in the earth realm has purpose for being here. We were born with the potential, gifts and talents that are to be discovered, developed, demonstrated, and deposited in the earth. We were designed and equipped to complete our assignment in the earth. We are not expected to carry any of our potential, gifts and talents, with us when we transition out of the earth. Opportunities and all types of resources are strategically placed to be available and accessible as needed to ensure our success. Because we are created in God's image and His likeness we have creative abilities and purpose. All of us were born to create our own success and make our way prosperous by observing to do all that's written in the Word of God and meditating in it day and night (Joshua 1:8; KJV) As you are blessed by reading this book, ask God the Father, in His Son Jesus' Name for clarity concerning His divine purpose for your life. Then joyfully and diligently develop and demonstrate the purpose He has designed and destined for you.

We are miraculously, wonderfully, and fashionably made with many individual, complex, and interdependent parts designed to transport our soul and human spirit throughout this world. Each part of the body does special jobs, but all the parts work together to make it run smoothly. Each cell has a purpose and responsibility to the rest of the body. We are spirit beings, living in the flesh with a soul that is comprised of the mind, emotions, will, and intellect.

Comparison of the Body to a Car

The physical body is the mode of transportation for our soul and spirit to contact this three-dimensional world during our earthly journey. Because of this, let's use the metaphor of a car. The human body is far more amazing than a car or any man-made machine, so the car metaphor is strictly to enhance comprehension. The Holy Spirit resides upon and within us as our Comforter, Counselor, Intercessor, Advocate, Helper, Strengthener, and Stand-by. So, the supernatural anointing of the Holy Spirit on our natural abilities makes tremendous power available to us.

Getting Ready for the Journey

Illustration 1 – **Body/Car Metaphor**

Car	Human Body
Manufacturer—authorized car dealer	Designer—Almighty God
Year designed	Conception
Fuel—gas	Food prepared according to age and ability to digest. Prayer is fuel for the soul
Paint—body work	Skin and Skin color.
Insurance—Must be renewed annually	Jesus Christ—Assurance (guarantee that has no expiration date)
Mechanics	Doctors, nurses, therapists, teachers, parents, and any source that helps to develop and/or keep the body in shape.
Chauffeur—driver	Holy Spirit
Passenger	Soul (mind, emotions, will, intellect)
Windows	Eyes
Motor	Belief
Electrical network	Nerves
Computer system	Brain
Transmission	Heart
Steering wheel	Mouth
Rims and tires	Legs and feet
Ignition	Faith
Keys	Redemption, righteousness, God's favor
Stabilik system	Wisdom and revelation knowledge
Gear selector	Trust
Oil and Lubricant	Love
Fuel tank	Liver
Oil filter	Kidneys
Air filtering system	Lungs
Combustion chamber	Digestive system
Chassis	Skeleton system
Battery	Tongue
Exhaust	Temper
Model	Body shape
Seat belt	Disciplined mind
Rear view Mirror	Your past
Windshield	Your future/vision
Horn	Praise
Key pad	Revelation knowledge
Road Map or GPS	Bible
Travel route	God's purpose for each individual
Highway	Life
Destination	Heaven—Final resting place

Referencing this metaphor will influence your comfort and competency levels as you passionately pursue and perform God's purpose for your life.

The Holy Spirit gives clarity concerning God's specific purpose. God is faithful to fulfill His promises and purposes for each of His children. I vividly recall how excited I was, and continue to be since the Holy Spirit has given me clarity concerning God's specific purpose for my life. I have grown to a deeper level spiritually and to a closer relationship with Christ with each platform of my God-given assignment in spite of the challenges. On one occasion, I was prayerfully preparing a speech to share as a keynote speaker at an annual district conference. As I was preparing the speech, I did not receive any inspiration for a closure and benediction. I always trust the Holy Spirit for revelation knowledge so while communicating with Him; I put the speech that I had begun to write aside and began to write on a clean sheet of paper. The content and Scriptures were the same as the speech that I had set aside, but the presentation of the information was changed. I was then inspired by the Holy Spirit to prepare the speech, using the metaphor comparing the human body to a car. At that time I knew very little about cars, but I was obedient to the Holy Spirit and shared the information with the audience as it had been divinely given to me.

The next day, a young lady approached me asking if I had spoken the previous day at the conference. The attendance at that conference was large so I immediately thought that she had attended but didn't get an opportunity to fellowship with me because of the long line. So, I asked if she had attended and she said no. Then tears filled her eyes as she told me that her brother had attended. She said that members of her family had been praying for him to get back in the church because he had been out for so long. Reportedly, upon request, her brother had brought some relatives to the conference. The distance was so far that instead of going home and then returning to get them, he attended the conference by sitting as far back as he could. But he wasn't too far for God to reach him. His sister and I were employed by the same organization, so when he returned home he asked her if she knew me. When she said yes, he proceeded to articulate to her the content, context, and his comfort level with the message. I then asked if he was a mechanic. When she said yes, I told her to please let her brother know that God loved him so much that He used me as the vessel to give him the information that he needed to know to grow spiritually.

This young lady began to attend all of my speaking engagements and tape record the messages for her brother. He would listen to them, and invite his friends to participate in a Bible study that he started in his home. Each week, they sat around the table with the recorder in the center as they listened, took notes, and had discussions on how to apply the information they learned from listening. Interestingly enough, later the young man did join the church and got hooked on the Word of God as he used study tapes of other lessons that God gave me. He continued to lead Bible studies in his home and boldly shared his testimony about how God reached out to him at the conference. During his Home-going ceremony after his transition out of this world, his pastor shared that testimony with all in attendance.

You don't have to be a mechanic to understand the aforementioned comparison. Be encouraged to get and apply the lessons. If you've ever seen, driven, or been a passenger in a car, you should have a general understanding of its purpose and what it takes to make it run efficiently. You should also understand that problems are always detectable and solvable. All cars come with manufacturers predetermined guidelines that give directions on preventive maintenance and problem solving so that you can receive the benefits of a high-performing vehicle. When we obey God's Word and always abide in Christ while responding in a timely and appropriate manner to the unction of the Holy Spirit, we will experience a successful enjoyable journey through life. The first step is to make the decision to choose to do so.

Chapter 2
Factors Influencing Decisions

Decisions are usually made based on the following factors:

- Will the results prove to be of immediate or future value for me and/or others?
- Will I continue to have a clear conscience without any feelings of guilt or wrongdoing?
- Do I have the freedom to make this decision independently, based on all the information that I know without offending anyone?
- Is there a need and opportunity to get more information?
- Am I making the decision of my own free will or because of the encouragement or demands someone else has made?
- A Christian will also want to know that the decision will please and glorify God.
- Am I confident that I have considered the conclusion of the whole matter and am making an informed decision?

The decisions you have made to date have influenced your current location. Is this where you expected to be in this season of your life? If so, did you have a plan and map that guided you? If not, where did you expect to be and why are you not there yet? Where are you going from here? Why? Now relate your answers to the discovery, development, and demonstration stages of God's purpose for your life.

The discovery, development and demonstration stages:

You will need a journal and pen for documenting your self assessment and progress through the completion of the three stages. The journal is only for you and not to be shared. This should give you the courage to be honest and transparent with yourself in a nonjudgmental way.

The self-discovery phase includes finding out the why of your existence, actions, decisions, passions and uniqueness. It includes assessing the gifts, talents, skill sets, culture and heritage of your current state of being. You will discover your uniqueness; what inspires you to do your best; whose opinion you value most; whether you function better independently or on teams; what pleases or displeases you; what makes you happy; what frustrates, worries or causes you to be anxious; how you respond when things don't go your way; what you enjoy doing and can do well with very little effort; why you feel and behave as you do; the things and people that cause you to be fearful, intimidated or doubt yourself. It's during this self awareness phase that you really get to know and understand you. The information that you get at this stage will provide a framework for the development phase. So it is important that you also identify your wish lists, priorities, daily schedule, current resources and knowledge level.

The development stage includes identifying your strengths and areas that you need to improve. Use the information in your journal that you learned during the discovery phase to develop a plan for you to grow spiritually, intellectually, and emotionally. In this stage you will develop your personal mission, vision and value statements that will serve as your compass for living. You will develop goals that are specific, measurable, attainable, realistic and time related (specify when the results can be achieved). Daily priority setting that incorporates meditation (time alone), acquiring new knowledge and stress release activities will prove to be an excellent investment of your time.

The demonstration stage is manifested when you apply what you learn to your circumstances, and environment as an intervention to effect the desired changes that you expect. You will begin to experience that you can create, change and control your circumstances. Knowledge is powerful only if you use it. If you don't apply the knowledge that you acquire then your results will be the same as the person who was never blessed with the knowledge.

In which of the three stages are you currently living? Picture yourself at the end of your life's journey and you have made your transition to your eternal resting place. Your name and two dates with a line between them are on your grave marker. The date before the line is your birth date, the date that you transitioned into this world. The date after the line is the date of your death, the date that you transitioned out of this world. So birth and death are passageways into and out of this world. As you think about this, what do you want others to remember most about you? In other words what information will be included in the line between your entry into and your exit out of this world? Have you fulfilled all of your dreams, visions, and plans? Are you on the path to do so? Are you currently pursuing with passion God's divine will and strategy for performing the purpose that He put in you prior to your arrival on earth? More importantly are you enjoying your life and your journey? God blesses all of us with the necessary resources to make our own way prosperous and successful (Joshua 1:6-8; KJV).

At birth, we are equipped with gifts, talents, and potential. As we grow and develop, we learn to appreciate the uniqueness and individuality of each person. With each level of maturity, we learn the value of lifelong learning. We come to understand that knowledge acquired, must be applied appropriately and timely in order to be powerful, effective, and efficient.

> Oh yes, you shaped me first inside, then out,
> you formed me in my mother's womb.
> I thank you, High God—you're breathtaking!
> Body and soul, I am marvelously made!
> I worship in adoration—what a creation!
> You know me inside and out,

you know every bone in my body;
You know exactly how I was made, bit by bit,
how I was sculpted from nothing into something.
Like an open book, you watched me grow from conception to birth;
all the stages of my life were spread out before you,
The days of my life all prepared
before I'd even lived one day.
(Psalms 139:13-16; MSG)

We were miraculously formed and knitted in the womb. We had no say in where, when, how, and to whom we would be born. However, God knew and also wrote every member of the body at conception and while in the embryo stage in His Book of Life. In fact, God knew us before we were conceived in our mother's womb, so as He knitted us in the womb He designed us with His purpose for our life in mind. He has a purpose that He wants to perform through each of us, and He designed us to fulfill that purpose. He made sure that our internal design, color, and body style included all the features and attributes needed to successfully transport our soul and spirit through life's journey.

The expectant mother must do her part as a co-partner with God to ensure that the embryo is nurtured and nourished. This is accomplished by eating right, getting appropriate exercise and health check-ups, following the doctor's orders, reading Scriptures, and speaking positive confessions to the baby in the womb. It is important to make preparation with great expectancy to receive the blessing (fruit of the womb) that will arrive at the appointed time. Included in the preparation is knowing when to leave for the birthing place, how to breathe during the labor contractions, and when to push down to press through to the blessing. Both parents should celebrate the arrival of their child to the earth and get excited about their role and responsibility in participating in the child's journey through life. It is also important those parents never cease to praise God for entrusting them to nurture and direct their child according to His Word. "Train up a child in the way he should go [and in keeping with his individual gift or bent], and when he is old he will not depart from it" (Proverbs 22:6; Amplified).

Children should be dedicated to the Lord and disciplined according to the Scriptures and God's purpose for their life. Occasionally, much time is wasted and disappointment occurs because children are not corrected according to the Scriptures but instead to popular opinion, relationships, and efforts made to recreate them in someone else' image.

> [4] Fathers, do not irritate *and* provoke your children to anger [do not exasperate them to resentment], but rear them [tenderly] in the training *and* discipline and the counsel *and* admonition of the Lord. (Ephesians 6:4; Amplified).

Chapter 3

Impregnated with God's Word

Just as a woman's pregnancy has an expected day of birth for the infant to be born, so does the Word of God have a date to be manifested in our life. We are impregnated with the Word of God when God's Word is in our hearts in abundance. The Word of God in our hearts should be meditated upon and should create expectancy within us. As the Word is established and takes root on the inside of our hearts and we believe it, then out of the abundance of our hearts we will speak into two places. We give God's Word back to Him in prayer, and we will speak that same Word over our circumstances that we desire to create, control, or change with that Word. The root system that anchors that spoken Word is from God's DNA (Divine Nature Assured), resulting from the measure of faith given to us and the love of God shed abroad in our hearts at the new birth, which is when we accept Jesus Christ as being made unto us our Redeemer, Sanctification, Righteousness and Wisdom. WOW (Wonder of Wonders), what an awesome God we serve. It is His nature to give us what we need to make our way prosperous and successful. God gave us the seed of His faith and His love because without faith it is impossible to please Him and faith will not work without love. So when we pray God's Word in Jesus' Name, we are echoing what God has already spoken about the outcome of the challenge that is being addressed and acknowledging that Christ as our intercessor in

Heaven will represent us with our Heavenly Father. As we speak that same Word to the disruptive, distracting, and difficult things in our circumstances in Jesus' Name, we are releasing the power of Christ to represent us in taking care of the situation on earth to ensure that we receive what God has promised to and purposed for us.

As the expectant parents prepare for the arrival of their baby, so we should prepare to receive full manifestation of our spoken words that are in agreement with God's Promises. Do not become distressed, discouraged, or depressed if the challenges seem unbearable or long. Let patience have her perfect work as you press your way through until the birth of your vision. Stay focused, faithful, and fervent in knowing that you will reap if you do not give up or become weary in well-doing. You do well to push through and not abort your vision or give up prematurely. Know that just as the newborn baby arrives in the earth with all the potential to perform God's purpose, so your vision has the potential to fulfill its purpose. Compare this analogy to the lesson that Christ was teaching His disciples about the potential in a grain of mustard seed to grow into a great big oak tree. The mustard seed's potential is released when it is planted in good, fertile soil (the correct environment) in the right season. After planting, the seed must be watered. After growth begins, the weeds must be kept out to prevent choking and measures taken to prevent the sun from drying out the tender plant. When the seed of the Word of God is planted in our hearts, it mixes with the faith and love that God placed there when we accepted Christ as our Lord and Savior. We should protect that seed from being choked by:

- other's opinions
- adverse circumstances
- unpleasant experiences
- stress
- anxiety
- worry
- man's traditions
- the cares of this world
- the deceitfulness of riches

Refuse to empower anyone or anything to:

- determine your confidence in God or yourself
- cause you to doubt
- steal your joy
- determine whether or not you will have a good or bad day
- rob you of any part of your destiny
- intimidate you
- overwhelm you
- hinder you from completing God's assignment
- prevent you from developing and performing your potential
- discourage you from optimizing your gifts and talents

Our obedience always results in blessings. Decisions governed by the Word of God bring us great joy and peace (nothing broken, missing, or lacking) in spite of the circumstances. Be determined to enjoy your trip through life.

Factors that Promote an Enjoyable Journey

As we journey through life from birth to death, we would enjoy the trip more once we understand that God decided our purpose and destiny before designing us. Therefore, we were designed to be successful before we were called into our earthly assignment.

> "God foreknew and predestined us to be conformed to the image of His Son that He might be the firstborn among many brethren. Moreover whom He did predestinate, them He also called: and whom He called, them He also justified: and whom He justified, them He also glorified" (Romans 8:28 31 KJV).

It is exciting to know that the works ensuring our success in fulfilling the purpose that God designed us for were "finished from the foundation of the world" (Heb 4:3b KJV).

God's purpose for each individual is an internal hidden treasure to be revealed later during the growth process God knows what's best and desires to give His best to us at all times. Christ died and was resurrected so that we could experience God's best. God has already proven just how much He loves us. He is faithful to fulfill His Promises and Covenant to all who trust Him to do so.

Chapter 4
Spiritual Growth Resources

Even though we are born to be happy and successful, it is a growth process and there are parents, teachers, family members, Godly friends, and others whom God had foreordained to be accessible and to answer for us. Before and after we reach the age of accountability (e.g., knowing right from wrong), God places people in our lives to educate, mentor, coach, and protect us as we grow toward spiritual maturity. He also ensures that adequate and appropriate physical resources are available as needed. Remember that we were created in His image and His likeness; therefore, there are no flaws in the way that God designed us to fulfill His purpose in each of us for His glory and our enjoyment. Know this: that enjoyment comes when efforts to please others are not a priority but pleasing God is. We should get comfortable and competent in expecting and receiving the God-kind of results as we speak His Word in prayer and over our circumstances in Jesus' Name. Anything that we want to create, control, or change can be accomplished by speaking God's Word in prayer and over our circumstances. God's Word spoken in heaven and on earth must be in agreement in both areas and relevant to the situation, experience, or circumstance in which we are being challenged. As it is written, God's Word must be spoken after it's believed; then the results are, and our expectations should be, that the power that God put in that Word when He first spoke it is released to perform what God had already spoken. Angels hearken to the voice of God's Word and are deployed and dispatched whenever a believer puts voice to God's Word. The Holy Spirit overshadows God's Word spoken by the believer in faith and projects it toward the goal. Once the goal is reached, the Holy Spirit releases the same power from that Word that God put in it when He first spoke it. God expects and we should expect God's Word to be performed to perfection just like God intended when He first spoke it.

Jesus Christ has already proven the effectiveness and efficiency of God's Words in all situations. Be reminded that Jesus the Son of God said that "... with God all things are possible" (Matthew 19:26). Gabriel, the chief messenger of all the angels said 'For with God nothing shall be impossible" (Luke 1:37) These are two valid and credible witnesses confirming the Scripture that states that it's by two or three witnesses that every word is established as truth.

With excitement, receive the God-kind of results. Get your expectations in line with God's Word, and speak only what you are expecting. Prepare to receive it when the full manifestation presents. Put a watch over your mouth, love, forgive, apply your faith, endure with patience, and guard your tongue, using it as the pen of a ready writer.

I recall when my youngest daughter Leah was seven years old. The Bible study group and Sunday School class members of the church that I attended at that time had planned to enjoy a picnic at Oak Mountain State Park in Alabama with lots of food, fun, and Christian fellowship

The goal was to enjoy each other in the Lord and show the younger members that Christians could and should have fun. We had planned the picnic over several months, and our special day had come with much enthusiasm and excitement. Well, we did not expect the forecast of rainy weather and thunderstorms. The forecast that Oak Mountain was included in the dismal weather forecast was predicted with certainty. Leah was determined not to be disappointed because, after all, she had envisioned a fun-filled day. Early the morning of the picnic, immediately after hearing the weather forecast, Leah looked at me and then said, "Mama, let's pray that it doesn't rain on our picnic." So naturally, I said, "Okay, let's do that." Leah prayed the following: "God, please don't let it rain on our picnic. We thank you in Jesus' name that it won't. Amen."

I said Amen and came into agreement with her faith-spoken words. At least that's what I thought at the time. So, we loaded up the car. As we were about to get in the car ourselves, I said, "Oops, Leah, wait a second, I forgot something." Leah asked "What did you forget Mama"? I said the umbrella. Leah responded by saying, "but we just prayed, and it is not going to rain on our picnic so we don't need an umbrella." I said, "That's right." All the way to Oak Mountain, Leah was excited, playing with her doll and chatting about how much fun we were going to have. The wind was blowing, and the sky was covered with very dark clouds. The weather man had interrupted the regular radio broadcast with a thunderstorm warning with high winds and a tornado watch for the area that we were traveling to. Leah heard it, looked at me and with glee said, "That does not include us because it is not going to rain on our picnic. Right, Mama?"

I responded with "That is so right, Leah." However, I whispered to God, "Okay, You are on and I know this is not too hard for You." Well, we arrived at the picnic area and everyone who attended had a great time. The dark clouds turned into a pleasant-looking overcast, and the roaring wind became a cool, refreshing breeze. It did not rain on our picnic. However, when we were leaving the park and came to the exit gates of Oak Mountain, we could see that it had rained and stormed all around the area leading to the gate and around the park, but it had not rained in the park because a little girl prayed in faith and with great expectancy. The spiritual laws that were activated and put into operation in this example included the power of agreement, the importance of adhering to and refusing to change your confession, and the assurance that God always answers prayer. Leah's prayer and confession also gives an example of how simple child-like faith always moves God and that all of His promises are yea and amen in Christ Jesus.

Principles for living in the Spirit include living in expectancy after you pray, preparing to receive, not focusing on or responding to any report that contradicts what you believe and confess, refusing to be intimidated by adverse circumstances or your inabilities, comparing the problem to God's all-sufficient grace (unmerited favor and enabling power), and refusing to doubt.

God will respond to faith-filled words that are spoken to Him, and things will respond to faith-filled words that are spoken to them. Because faith echoes God's Word back to Him, God responds by sending the answer back through some of those Words spoken to Him in prayer. Directional, faith-filled words provide a spiritual highway to transport God's answer to our prayers and confessions back to us. Our faith is demonstrated when our actions are aligned with our expectations. In other words, we respond by preparing to receive complete manifestation of answered prayer to confirm our confidence, knowing that God can and will do what He has promised in His Word.

As the expectant mother prepares for the arrival of her baby, so should we prepare to receive answers to prayer whenever we pray. Preparation includes everything that we do to show that we sincerely believe that we have what we prayed for before the results are manifested (brilliantly seen). Lots of things have to happen prior to the birth of the baby. So, even though there may be uncomfortable experiences, morning sickness, bodily changes, and emotional roller coaster challenges during pregnancy, it is very exciting to share the joy with others in making sure that everything is ready for the arrival of the expected new family member. So when the baby arrives, the celebration that began when it was announced that the baby was coming is continued with much praise and thanksgiving. Everything and everybody that was prepared for the arrival is ready to receive with excitement and enjoy this wonderful blessing of the fruit of the womb. The pregnant mother is sometimes unaware that she is carrying a blessing until she is informed by her physician. Sometimes because of various and sundry reasons, she keeps it a secret until later.

Sometimes those who are pregnant don't always tell others about it until there's physical manifestation in their body. They keep it a secret for a variety of reasons. Likewise, some people pray in secret and never tell anyone until they can see, feel, touch or hear something in their surroundings as evidence to them that God has heard and is answering their prayers. Their experiences have more influence than their faith in determining their level of joy.

The experience with previous pregnancies may influence whether or not the current pregnancy will be kept a secret or not. Previous challenges in conception, a problem with carrying a baby full term, worry about the baby being accepted or concern about available resources to care for the baby may encourage keeping the pregnancy a secret.

Likewise, previous unexpected experiences with telling others about what you are praying for may convince you to keep certain prayers a secret. Those experiences may include dealing with personalities that are not at your level of spiritual growth so they think that your prayer will not be answered, or that you are asking God for something that in the natural that is impossible for you to have, be or do. In these cases joy is influenced by faith and living in the promises of God rather than the opinion of others.

Prayer is the communication system between God and man. , God heareth the prayers of the righteous (Prov 15:29). The righteous cry, and the LORD heareth, and delivereth them out of all their troubles (Ps 34:17). Jesus said that... "when you pray to thy Father which is in secret; and thy Father which seeth in secret shall reward thee openly."(Matthew 6:6)"

So, whether you pray openly or in secret in faith believe that God heareth, and answereth. Know that.... the desire of the righteous shall be granted (Prov. 10:24). Our desires are created and sustained by God's Word which is His Will. It is God's Will that all men are to be saved and come unto the knowledge of the truth (God's Word I Tim 2:4). Jesus defined the truth as God's Word (John 17:17). Therefore, we can pray God's Word openly or in secret. It is great joy in heaven and on earth when people are saved and learn God's Word

The excitement and joy of all blessings will continue throughout life's journey if you do the following:

- Make the decision to enjoy your trip to your destiny.
- Search the Scriptures Because in them ye think ye have eternal life; but it is the Scriptures that bear witness of Christ (John 5:39; KJV). Christ defined eternal life as knowing God, the Father and Jesus Christ (John 17:3; KJV)

- Be committed to developing, nurturing, and maintaining a close personal relationship with God, who is the source of life. The life being referenced involves more than just breathing, having no goals, not being productive and tossed to and fro by others' opinions of you. The God-kind of life (Zoe) rooted in the Word of God is productive and prosperous, in spite of the challenges. Man's source of life is God. (God breathed into Adam and Eve, and they became living souls.) The Bible defines death as separation from the source of life. A fish taken out of water, a plant uprooted from the soil and laid aside, and a branch separated from the tree or vine soon eventually dies. Because God is man's source of life, separation from Him results in spiritual death. So, in order to experience the God kind of life (Zoe) and experience His best, there must be repentance, confession, and acceptance of God's salvation plan. At the new spiritual birth, Jesus became our source of the redemptive life, and the Holy Spirit lives on the inside of each believer so He that is in us is greater than he that is in the world. (1 John 4:4; KJV)
- Confess only those words over yourself, your loved ones, and your circumstances that agree with what God has already said about them as revealed in the Bible that reveals all the promises of God.
- If, and when necessary, know how to encourage yourself in the Lord in all seasons.

Seasons of physical life are identifiable by the chronological age and development age. Spiritual life seasons are determined by one's spiritual development and level of faith maturity. Below is a list of prerequisite questions to encourage you to prepare for identifying your level of spiritual growth prior to going through the Spiritual Growth Study.

Prerequisite Questions to the Christian Growth Study

1. Just where am I in the spiritual growth process?

2. What is my frame of reference? Considering the date and time that I accepted Jesus as my Lord and Savior, how has my life changed?
3. What is my knowledge of the Bible? What is that knowledge based on?
4. How often do I make applications of the Scriptures in my life?
5. Do my prayer life and daily conversation reflect my knowledge of the Scriptures?
6. Am I the victor or the victim in my circumstances?
7. Am I an overcomer or often overwhelmed by my experiences?
8. Am I a praiser or do I throw frequent pity-parties?
9. Am I a tither or a miser?
10. Do I consistently behave as more than a conqueror or a chronic complainer?
11. Do I speak words of power or defeat?
12. Do I throw temper tantrums or do I demonstrate patience and self-control?
13. Do I speak as one having the trained tongue of the learned whose speech is with salt seasoned with grace so that I know how I ought to answer every man?
14. Am I a good steward of God's blessings? Can I be trusted at all times to represent Christ as a good follower and ambassador?
15. Am I willing to forgive myself and others?
16. Am I using my gifts and talents constructively?
17. What is the driving force of my life?
18. What am I here for?
19. Do I need more silence and solitude?
20. Are my priorities in order?
21. When my life is over, will I have made a difference?

Answering these questions is a prerequisite to the "Levels and Characteristics of Spiritual Growth Study".

> Spiritual development must occur just like physical development. Both require a balanced diet of the right kind of food.

Now that you have answered the previous questions, you should be mentally, emotionally, and spiritually prepared to study the spiritual growth chart in the next chapter. As you prayerfully identify your current level of spiritual growth, be encouraged and get excited about taking action to progress to the next level. Be committed to continue to grow in faith.

Chapter 5

Levels and Characteristics of Spiritual Growth

The Scriptures list babyhood, childhood and manhood as the three levels of Spiritual Growth. In the chart below, I refer to those as infancy, children and adult levels. I also added Adolescent as a fourth level. Acquired wisdom validates to me that characteristics of spiritual growth mirrors physical growth. I acquired this wisdom from studying Scripture and observations as a mother, grandmother, experienced pediatric nurse and anointed bible teacher. Following is a chart for you to do a self assessment to identify your current level of spiritual growth. Pray as you complete your personal assessment and be encouraged to develop and follow a plan to progress to the next level.

Illustration 2 – **Levels of Spiritual Growth** (Infants)

Level	Characteristics	Scripture
Infants Satisfiers: Bottle with milk, nipple and a little cereal. Pacifies, rattlers, flashing colors, noise, bright light, pleasant sounds, and familiarity. Babies should be weaned; but, some organizations are full of breast or bottle fed babies who have temper tantrums if they can't get their way on what they're used to. Requires a pacifier to be content. Don't understand that they are a separate person Turns toward familiar sounds and voices Enjoys being talked to or played with Immature visual image Main form of communicating is crying	Blameless-. No past. Receive assurance that God has forgiven you completely. **Inexperienced & unskilled** in application of God's Word. Must be bottle or breast fed. Bonding and voice recognition occurs. Learn understanding of love and it's security **Unlearned-** (everything found or experienced in the environment goes into the mouth) Doesn't know what should or should not go into their mouths. Vulnerable to false doctrines (poisonous). Poison is usually mixed with good food e.g. the devil mixes good scripture with poison. **Fretful** (easily spoiled, distracted, easily frustrated, easily hurt) Things have to be what they've become used to (e.g. lights on all nights, etc.) Likes to be held, pampered, stroked, loved, etc. Totally dependent Lack of discernment	II Cor. 5:17- therefore if any man is in Christ, he is a new creature…(KJV) I Peter 2:2 – Desires and requires milk. Requires feeding; attention & is accountable to some adult. Romans 5:5; 12:3 At new birth we receive God's grace, the measure of faith and the love of God is shed abroad in our hearts. Prov 7:24 reminds us to be careful what you read (feed upon). You become like that you attend to. You are what you eat/read. Ps 131:2 - I've kept my feet on the ground, I've cultivated a quiet heart. Like a baby content in its mother's arms, my soul is a baby content. *(Message)* Heb 5:13 - For everyone who continues to feed on milk is obviously inexperienced and unskilled in the doctrine of righteousness (of conformity to the divine will in purpose, thought, and action), for he is a mere infant [not able to talk yet - Amplified

Levels and Characteristics of Spiritual Growth

Illustration 2 – **Levels of Spiritual Growth** (Children)

Level	Characteristics	Scripture
Children Immature and not dependable. Will begin a task but not complete it if something more interesting competes with it (going to the beach with friends, washing the car, mowing the lawn, playing golf, going fishing, etc. instead of going to church, Sunday school, bible study, prayer meeting. Interacts in different ways at different times with a different playmate Learns how to develop relationships	Wavering, inquiring Undeveloped spiritually, self-centeredness, pretenders, manipulative, need guidance, teachable, trusting, enthusiastic, imitators, sporadic Untrustworthy Unprofitable speaking- **Self-Centeredness** - Always speaking about self. Where I've been, What I have, What I'm going to do, What I've done- proud & boastful **Offensive speaking** (making hateful, disrespectful, insulting and rude comments about others Discussing the mistakes, character weakness and personal shortcomings of others Speaking injurious words against another Tossed to and fro trying to be popular Wants to know what's going on. Very gossipy.- spread rumors Always poking their noses in other peoples' business Self Pity Needs approval, praise and encouragement	Ephesians 4:14-15-No prolonged infancies among us, please. We'll not tolerate babes in the woods, small children who are an easy mark for impostors. God wants us to grow up, to know the whole truth and tell it in love—like Christ in everything. (Message) Ephesians 5:4 -Though some tongues just love the taste of gossip, Christians have better uses for language than that. Don't talk dirty or silly. That kind of talk doesn't fit our style. Thanksgiving is our dialect. (Message) Proverbs 10:19 -The more talk, the less truth; the wise measure their words (Message) 2 Timothy 2:14 - Of these things put *them* in remembrance, charging *them* before the Lord that they strive not about words to no profit, *but* to the subverting of the hearers. (KJV) Titus 2:3 ...To speak evil of no man, to be no brawlers, but gentle, showing all meekness unto all men. Jer. 9:23-24-God's Message: "Don't let the wise brag of their wisdom. Don't let heroes brag of their exploits. Don't let the rich brag of their riches. If you brag, brag of this and this only: That you understand and know me. I'm God, and I act in loyal love. I do what's right and set things right and fair, and delight in those who do the same things. These are my trademarks." God's Decree. (Message)

Illustration 2 – **Levels of Spiritual Growth (Adolescent)**

Level	Characteristics	Scriptures
Adolescent (Group Think) Invulnerability	Rebellious against authority. Wants to form little groups or be part of one. Very competitive. Misaligned expectations. Impulsive, intense, Idealistic, Immediate (wanting everything now), Indestructible (thinking nothing can hurt them	Hebrews 13:17 - Obey them that have the rule over you, and submit yourselves: for they watch for your souls, as they that must give account, that they may do it with joy, and not with grief: for that is unprofitable for you.(KJV)
	Asserts independence from family, increasing ability to compromise; increasing independence and decision making; experiments to determine self image; graffiti, cliques; builds a personal set of values; a personal sense of morality; starts to make lasting friendships; have wider interests; employs abstract thinking; has increase mobility; present- oriented, easily and often disappointed; doesn't consider the consequences of all decisions Moody, messy, Money-oriented, me-centered, Believe that their personal problems, feelings, and experiences are unique to them. Tend to be self-conscious, lacking in self-esteem, and highly sensitive to criticism	Read a chapter in Proverbs daily Exodus 20:12- Regard (treat with honor, due obedience, and courtesy) your father and mother, that your days may be long in the land the Lord your God gives you (Amplified Bible)

Levels and Characteristics of Spiritual Growth

Illustration 2 – **Levels of Spiritual Growth (Adult)**

Level	Characteristics	Scriptures
Adulthood - Keys to Kingdom: (1) Redemption through Jesus Christ (2) Resisting the devil and (3) righteousness of God Birth certificate: Created in God's image and His likeness. Ability to work for, buy, prepare and eat. Jas 1:19-26, Hearer and doer of God's Word. Looks in the mirror (Bible) often Jas 1:26; Heb 13:6; Ps 118:6 Know the value of bridling the tongue. I Cor 9:27- Brings flesh/body under subjection. I Cor; 10:13-14 – Trust God to make a way/be a way of escape from temptation. Jas 1:13-15- Knows 7 steps of sliding into sin. II Pet 2:9 – Expects God to deliver the Godly out of temptation. Redemption – Deliverance from danger, destruction, oppression and captivity. (I Cor 15:57 -Thanks be to God which giveth us the victory through our Lord Jesus Christ. (KJV)	Puts Spiritual things above earthly things Not influenced or affected by what others think of him/her Governed by the law of love Not easily puffed up, nor touchy or resentful Pays no account to the evil done to them Dominated by the Spirit of God: sensitive and responsive to the Holy Spirit God Conscious- Ever conscious of what God's Word says to and bout them Recognizes the source of evil and works of the devil Ability to resist the devil steadfast in the faith Overcomer by faith, word of our testimony and the Blood of the Lamb Ability to recognize God's Ways (Isa 55:8-11) Enjoys fellowshipping with other believers Knows what belongs to him/her in Christ Jesus and takes advantage of it/lives by it. Comes to know the	Hebrews 11:24-26 -By faith, Moses, when growing, refused the privileges of the Egyptian royal house. He chose a hard life with God's people rather than an opportunistic soft life of sin with the oppressors. He valued suffering in the Messiah's camp far greater than Egyptian wealth because he was looking ahead, anticipating the payoff. (Message) III John 2- Beloved, I wish above all things that thou mayest prosper and be in health, even as thy soul prospereth (KJV) Psalms 1:1-3 – Blessed is the man that walketh not in the counsel of the unGodly, nor standeth in the way of sinners, nor sitteth in the seat of the scornful. [2] But his delight is in the law of the LORD; and in his law doth he meditate day and night. [3] And he shall be like a tree planted by the rivers of water, that bringeth forth his fruit in his season; his leaf also shall not wither; and whatsoever he doeth shall prosper. (KJV) II Cor. 1:20 – For all the promises of God in him *are* yea,and in him Amen unto the glory of God by us (KJV)

Illustration 2 – **Levels of Spiritual Growth (Adult)**

Level	Characteristics	Scriptures
Adulthood - Keys to Kingdom: (cont)	Son, Lord Jesus Christ in His great ministry at the right hand of God (e.g. as High Priest, advocate, intercessor, Shepherd, Lord).	
	Knows the Holy Spirit as He is unveiled in the Word: (e.g. as indweller, Greater One in us, teacher). Knows his inheritance and know how to enjoy it.	I Cor 4:3-4-The requirements for a good guide are reliability and accurate knowledge. It matters very little to me what you think of me, even less where I rank in popular opinion. I don't even rank myself. Comparisons in these matters are pointless. I'm not aware of anything that would disqualify me from being a good guide for you, but that doesn't mean much. The Master makes that judgment. (Message)
	Knows that God is our ability.	
	Governed by the Word of God.	
	Lives by faith (according to God's Word) and not by sight (the senses or the flesh	
	Walk in the newness of life	I Cor 13: The qualities of Godly love (KJV)
	Walks in the Spirit and shall not fulfill the lust of the flesh	Ps 119:130-The entrance of God's Word giveth life (KJV)
	Comply with, concur, confidence in the scriptures	Prov 20:27- The spirit of man is the candle of the Lord.(KJV)
		Ps 18:28-For thou will light my candle: the LORD my God will enlighten my darkness (KJV)
		Heb 10:35- Cast not away therefore your confidence, which hath great recompense of reward (JKV)

Levels and Characteristics of Spiritual Growth

Illustration 2 – **Levels of Spiritual Growth (Adult)**

Level	**Characteristics**	**Scriptures**
Adulthood (con't) *Knows what causes backsliding, err, and destruction*	Can rejoice no matter what is going on Quickly repents, ask forgiveness, receives forgiveness and forgives others Consistently pays tithes and gives offerings Refuses to follow false shepherds and leaders who err Insensitive to criticism or praise (not moved by either) Knows why Christ was manifested. Knows God as light, deliverer and strength of life Soul is anchored in Jesus Stable at all times because of wisdom, knowledge and strength of salvation Experienced in creating, controlling and changing circumstances by meditating, praying, and confessing the Word of God that's relevant to addressing the issue	I John 1:8-9 - If we say that we have no sin, we deceive ourselves, and the truth is not in us. If we confess our sins, he is faithful and just to forgive us our sins, and to cleanse us from all unrighteousness.(KJV) Isa 9:16- For the leaders of this people cause them to err; and they that are led of them are destroyed. (KJV) Heb 13:5-6 (KJV) Heb 6:17-19 (KJV) Isa 33:6 And wisdom and knowledge shall be the stability of thy times, and strength of salvation (KJV) Understand the power available in Jesus name. Know how to pray requests in Jesus Name and speak His name over circumstances Jn 14:13; Jn 16:23 (KJV)

According to Ecclesiastes 3:1-2, "To everything there is a season, and a time to every purpose under the heaven: A time to be born, and a time to die; a time to plant, and a time to pluck up *that which is* planted" (KJV). From this statement it is evident from the examination of God's character in reference to the information about the stages of spiritual growth that:

- All the events of history including our lives occur according to God's timetable and purpose.
- God is all-knowing and He knows the beginning and end of all things.
- God is the One who causes all things to happen in their "seasons" and gives everything purpose.

The *spring season* of growth is during the youth period when the root, value, and moral systems are being developed. Balanced educational activities, according to the Scriptures and academic institutions, are also prevalent. Adulthood exemplifies the *summer season* of our life. This places emphasis on building and demonstrating a Christ-like character by applying knowledge to live consistently in the victory and overcoming challenges and obstacles. We become infallible proof that God is faithful to always perform His Word.

The golden years are indicative of the *autumn season* of life. These are the years in which there is a complete understanding of how to be effective and efficient in creating success (e.g., the ability to skillfully apply God's Word appropriately and timely). One can thoroughly apply knowledge of God's purpose for his or her life. There's enjoyment and zeal for nurturing and nourishing self and others to be, do, and live in God's best. It's in the *autumn season* that expertise and experiences learned over the years are offered to others through training, mentoring, and coaching to teach them how to be successful in spite of difficulties.

The *winter season* is characterized by a state of readiness, awareness, and sensitivity to the importance of putting everything in order for the transition out of this world. This includes sharing with significant others what they need to know. It is important to remember that there is a transition from each season of life and level of spiritual growth. However, certain characteristics and traits overlap and are not necessarily independent for a certain season or particular level of growth.

With each level of spiritual growth, a transformation occurs by the renewal of your mind as you study and develop spiritually according to the Word of God. Transformation is a radical change in one's inner character, condition, or nature. As followers of Christ, we should not be conformed, either inwardly or in appearance, to the values, ideals, and behavior of a fallen world.

Don't consent to being squeezed into this world's mold, and don't be confined to its fears, limitations, doubts, and unbelief. As believers, we should continually renew our minds through prayer and the study of God's Word by the power of the Holy Spirit, and so be transformed and made like Christ. Our spiritual growth level and season in life is influenced by our relationships, attitudes, behaviors, traveling companions, travel plans, scheduled events, places visited, suitable age-appropriate clothing, weather, circumstances of life, and destination. So what is your destination? There are only two options. They are heaven or hell, and preparation occurs during your earthly journey. After transition from earthly travels, you will reside in the designated place that you chose, prepared for, and traveled to. Remember that your preparation will determine your destination. Also, preparation before performance positions you to be established in a state of readiness for success, especially when opportunity shows up at your address.

Chapter 6

A Three-Step Return on Investment (ROI) Process

Sacrifice/Counting the Cost

Prior to traveling to any place, a wise person usually gathers information, and considers the cost compared to the benefits of going. In the secular world, this process is known as calculating the return on investment (ROI). This calculation involves a three-step process:

1. **Calculate all the costs associated with an investment**
   - Initial upfront cost
   - Maintenance costs
   - Any fees or associated taxes
   - Research cost
   - Your time
   - Hidden cost

2. **Estimate or calculate your returns**
   - How much do you expect to gain from the investment?
   - When do you expect returns to happen?

- o Detail specifically all the individual returns you expect to receive from the investments.
- o Know the certainty of the ROI in God's kingdom so you don't have to worry about the probability of each return if you have developed and understood how to demonstrate your faith.

3. **Establish a timeline for costs and returns.**
   - o Keep a journal.
   - o Draw a simple timeline or just list in chronological order all the costs and returns you discovered in steps 1 and 2

Christ shared His formula for the cost of discipleship by giving two examples in Luke 14:28-33:

> Is there anyone here who, planning to build a new house, doesn't first sit down and figure the cost so you'll know if you can complete it?
>
> If you only get the foundation laid and then run out of money, you're going to look pretty foolish.
>
> Everyone passing by will poke fun at you:
>
> 'He started something he couldn't finish.'
>
> "Or can you imagine a king going into battle against another king without first deciding whether it is possible with his ten thousand troops to face the twenty thousand troops of the other?
>
> And if he decides he can't, won't he send an emissary and work out a truce?
>
> "Simply put, if you're not willing to take what is dearest to you, whether plans or people, and kiss it good-bye, you can't be my disciple" (The MSG Bible).

In these two illustrations, Christ was emphasizing that to be one of His disciples required a sacrifice and an awareness of the cost of the investment. Christ taught His disciples principles out of the Word of God while encouraging and expecting then to transform their thinking, change their attitude, and conform their behavior to align to what He taught them.

Return on Investment (ROI)-

ROI = Benefits / Cost. Current Cost–Cost after change or intervention = Benefits

Cost includes sacrifice of something valued (e.g. time, talent, treasures)

In calculating the ROI for God's work as a disciple of Christ, each individual will include their spiritual gifts, talents, time, treasures, faith level, and spiritual growth stage in the formula.

"**Talent**," like "pound," is used metaphorically in the New Testament for mental and spiritual attainments or gifts (see Matthew 25:15-28). According to Strong's Hebrew and Greek Dictionary, talent is also a *balance* (as *supporting* weights), that is, (by implication) a certain *weight* (and thence a *coin* or rather *sum* of money).

Time signifies a fixed or definite period, a season, or opportunity.

Treasure is "the light of the knowledge of the glory of God in the face of Jesus Christ. Descriptive of the Gospel as deposited in the earthen vessels of the persons who proclaim it" (2 Corinthians 4:6, 7). Note, too, that all the treasures of "wisdom and knowledge are hidden in Christ" (Colossians 2:3).

As you add these values in the formula remember this:

"A man's *gift* maketh room for him, and bringeth him before great men" (Proverbs 18:16 KJV). God's Divine Nature assured (DNA) is the love of God and the measure of faith (Romans 12:3; 5:5 KJV). According to Ephesians 4:10-15

He who descended is the same as He who ascended again far above all the Heavens in order to fill the universe.) And He Himself appointed some to be Apostles, some to be Prophets, some to be evangelists, some to be pastors and teachers, in order fully to equip His people for the work of serving—for the building up of Christ's body—till we all of us arrive at oneness in faith and in the knowledge of the Son of God, and at mature manhood and the stature of full-grown men in Christ. So we shall no longer be babes nor shall we resemble mariners tossed on the waves and carried about with every changing wind of doctrine according to men's cleverness and unscrupulous cunning, making use of every shifting device to mislead. But we shall lovingly hold to the truth, and shall in all respects grow up into union with Him who is our Head, even Christ.

Dependent on Him, the whole body—its various parts closely fitting and firmly adhering to one another—grows by the aid of every contributory link, with power proportioned to the need of each individual part, so as to build itself up in a spirit of love" (New Testament in Modern Speech, Ed. 1).

Love is essential to faith because in Jesus Christ ...faith worketh by love (Gal 5:6 KJV). God has dealt to every man the measure of faith (Rom 12:3-KJV). The love of God is shed abroad in our hearts by the Holy Ghost which is given to us (Rom 5:5 KJV). Our Awesome God has blessed us with what we need to please him and access resources from the Kingdom of Heaven according to His Will and purpose for each of us. Without faith, it is impossible to please God for he who cometh (approach or come near) to Him, must believe that he is, and that he is a rewarder of them that diligently seek-(stand in awe of) him. (Heb 11:6-KJV emphasis mine)

There are levels, attributes and degrees of faith

Levels of faith—"God hath dealt to every man the measure of faith" (Romans 12:3). Note the comparison of translations for Hebrews 11:1 as follows:

- Now faith is the substance of things hoped for, the evidence of things not seen. (KJV)
- Now faith is the assurance of things hoped for, the conviction of things not seen. (NASB)
- Now faith is the assurance (the confirmation, the title—deed) of the things [we] hope for, being the proof of things [we] do not see and the conviction of their reality—faith perceiving as real fact what is not revealed to the senses. (AMP)
- Now faith is being sure of what we hope for and certain of what we do not see. (NIV)
- Faith is the confident assurance that something we want is going to happen. It is the certainty that what we hope for is waiting for us even though we cannot see it up ahead (The Living Bible)
- The fundamental fact of existence is that this trust in God, this faith, is the firm foundation under everything that makes life worth living. It's our handle on what we can't see. The act of faith is what distinguished our ancestors, set them above the crowd. (Message)

Faith lays hold of the unseen real hope and bringing it into reality. People often do not receive the answers to their prayer because they are only hoping they will receive (healing job, financial blessings, etc.). Prayer does not change God, it changes circumstances.

Christ described the **levels of faith** as follows:

No faith—Full of fear and focused on the circumstances (Mark 4:35-41)

Little faith—Misunderstanding, misinterpreting, and thusly wrongly dividing and applying the Word of God (Matthew 16:8-10).

Great Faith—Knows and speaks the authority of God's Word, expecting it to be performed when spoken. (Matt 8:5-10). Faith says it is mine; I have it now. Hope says, I'll get it sometime. As long as you are in hope and not in faith, whatever it is you desire will never materialize—it will never come into being. But the moment you start believing, confessing, and acting like God's Word is so, your faith will work for you.

Attributes of Faith

Faith is:

A gift—God gave us the measure of faith at the new birth (Romans 12:3).

Spirit—We having the same spirit of faith, according as it is written, I believed, and therefore have I spoken: we also believe and therefore speak. God is Spirit. God's Word is Spirit and Truth. So, our faith gives us confidence to know, believe, confess and receive the Promises of God. (Psalm 116:10; 2 Corinthians 4:13)

Seed—So must be sown in good ground (a heart that is prepared through prayer to receive the incorruptible seed of the Word of God). Sowing the Word of God in good ground will result in a thirty, sixty, or hundred-fold harvest.

The substance—It is the confirmation, assurance, the title deed of the things we hope for and proof, firm foundation of the unseen things that we are believing in God to make a reality.

Stability—And there shall be stability in your times, an abundance of salvation, wisdom, and knowledge; the reverent fear *and* worship of the Lord is your treasure *and* His. (Isaiah 33:6; AMP)

A Three-Step Return on Investment (ROI) Process

The Spiritual Growth Chart will guide you in your personal development and in completing the formula for your ROI.

After you calculate the cost, input the investments into the formula while reviewing and understanding the benefits as explained in the Scriptures. Note the following definitions:

> **Investment—contribution to activity:** a contribution of something such as time, energy, or effort to an activity, project, or undertaking in the expectation of a benefit (Encarta Dictionary: English)
>
> **Sacrifice—giving up of something valued:** a giving up of something valuable or important for somebody or something else considered to be of more value or importance (Encarta Dictionary: English)

Some Scriptures reminding us of God's benefits are:

> Psalm 68:19—Blessed *be* the Lord, *who* daily loadeth us *with benefits, even* the God of our salvation. *Selah* (KJV)
>
> Psalm 103:1-6—Bless the LORD, O my soul: and all that is within me, *bless* his holy name. Bless the LORD, O my soul, and forget not all his benefits: Who forgiveth all thine iniquities; who healeth all thy diseases; Who redeemeth thy life from destruction; who crowneth thee with loving kindness and tender mercies; Who satisfieth thy mouth with good *things; so that* thy youth is renewed like the eagle's. The LORD executeth righteousness and judgment for all that are oppressed. (KJV)

There are many more Scriptures explaining God's benefit package accessible for all those who obey Him. Be blessed by engaging in a thorough research or study of all of them expecting the Holy Spirit to give you revelation knowledge that you can apply in your daily decision making. All Scripture that addresses the grace, goodness, favor, pleasure, liberality, and acceptable will of God gives us valuable information about God's benefit package. You will discover the joy in knowing that being an investor in the Kingdom of God ensures a thirty-, sixty-, or hundredfold return.

Chapter 7
Unexpected Roadblocks

Now that you have calculated your ROI and confident that God's benefit package is accessible to you, be determined to do your part to ensure that you receive all the promised blessings therein. Most people prepare for the expected and get discomfited, discouraged, distressed, or even depressed because of unexpected temporary obstructions, obstacles, barricades, barriers, or blockades. These temporary and unexpected roadblocks must be addressed immediately upon identification. If not, they will distract and derail progress, hinder growth and productivity as well as interfere with successfully reaching your destination in a timely fashion. More importantly, it could influence whether or not you enjoy your trip to your destination (e.g., heaven).

Self-imposed Roadblocks

Unwise choices, disobeying God's Word, being unequally yoked, stubbornness, unforgiveness, resentment, self pity, judging others, indifference, anxiety, playing the blame game, fear, lack of faith, bitterness, anger, ignorance of God's Word, unmanaged stress and intimidation (failure to apply God's Word in what we know to do) are all self-imposed roadblocks on our journey.

Some of the unexpected situations result from inadequate stress management. The American Medical Association defines stress as any interference that disturbs a person's mental or physical well-being. Stress affects the mind, body, and behavior in many ways, and everyone experiences it differently. Stress doesn't always look stressful. Psychologist Dr. Connie Lillas uses a driving analogy to describe the three most common ways people respond when they're overwhelmed by stress:

- **Foot on the gas**—An angry or agitated stress response. You're heated, keyed up, overly emotional, and unable to sit still.
- **Foot on the brake**—A withdrawn or depressed stress response. You shut down, space out, and show very little energy or emotion.
- **Foot on both**—A tense and frozen stress response. You "freeze" under pressure and can't do anything. You look paralyzed, but under the surface you're extremely agitated.

According to Dr. Lillas, once one loses the balance of being in a calm and present state, one's stress responses (at any age) go into one of three primary directions:

- "Too hot" stress response—acceleration of the nervous system such as frustration or anger.
- "Too cold" stress response—shutting down and tuning out behaviors.
- "Mix" of hot and cold stress responses—blend of out-of-balance behaviors, including anxious withdrawal, anxious clinging, or being hyper-vigilant.

If not managed, excess stress will make you a victim of toxic emotions, mental instability, and it will negatively affect your health and well-being. Toxic emotions caused by stress overload can rob you of life, health, and joy. Some powerful remedies on how to minimize and manage stress include the following:

1. Getting good nutrition, exercise, sleep
2. Praying the promises of God
3. Studying and applying and speaking relevant Scriptures to your situation—2 Timothy 2:15

   Do not let your hearts be troubled, neither let them be afraid. (Stop allowing yourselves to be agitated and disturbed: and do not permit yourselves to be fearful and intimidated and cowardly and unsettled" (John 14:27; AMP).

The following chart summarizes why laughter and the joy of the Lord is good medicine to decrease stress.

Illustration 3 - Laughter

Remedy	Scripture
Laughter and the restorative strength of joy. A merry heart is your greatest weapon against deadly emotions. Laughter holds as much healing power as medicine. Those whose laugh easily often live longer than those who do not.	Prov 17:22—"A merry heart doeth good *like* a medicine: but a broken spirit drieth the bones."
A person who is happy and at peace with himself and his surroundings have significantly fewer illnesses than the unhappy person. Professor Norman Cousins, author, editor, journalist, writer, and speaker laughed himself into health after being diagnosed with an incurable illness. He read about the theory that negative emotions are harmful to the body, so he thought that if negative emotions were detrimental to health, then positive emotions should improve health. He checked himself out of the hospital and into a Manhattan hotel suite. He hired a nurse who read humorous stories and played Marx Brothers movies for him. Norman Cousins discovered that twenty minutes of hearty belly laughs could give him two hours of pain free sleep. Hearty laughter is also supposed to be a good work out for the heart and stimulation for good blood circulation and the immune system. His conclusion was that laughter, happiness, and joy are perfect antidotes for stress. By 1989 an article entitled "Laugh if This Is a Joke" in the Journal of the American Medical Association (JAMA) agreed that laughter therapy could improve the quality of life for patients with chronic illnesses. The positive effects of laughter are relief or improvement of the symptoms of disease. According to a 1988 Health Update published in *The New York Times,* A family practitioner at New Jersey's School of Osteopathic Medicine, Dr. Marvin E. Herring, said, "The diaphragm, thorax, abdomen, heart, lungs and even the liver are given a massage during a hearty laugh." And Dr. William F. Fry of Stanford University said that "laughter stimulates the production of the alertness hormones catecholamines. These hormones in	Isa 26:3—"Thou wilt keep him in perfect peace, whose mind is stayed on thee: because he trusteth in thee." Isa 61:3—". . . to give unto them beauty for ashes, the oil of joy for mourning, the garment of praise for the spirit of heaviness; . . ." Isa 12:2—"Behold, God is my salvation; I will trust, and not be afraid: for the LORD JEHOVAH is my strength and my song; he also is become my salvation."

Laughter Illustration 3

Remedy	Scripture
turn cause the release of endorphins in the brain. Endorphins foster a sense of relaxation and well-being and dull the perception of pain."	
. . . for the joy of the LORD is your strength. Never give up or be robbed of your joy.	Neh 8:10
Laugher is good medicine; a Swedish study says—Published in the Birmingham News-Health/Science section Tuesday Jan 31, 1989.	
A merry heart maketh a cheerful countenance; A person with a merry heart has a continual feast (regardless of circumstances).	Prov 15:13, 15 (Amp)
Live a life in joy and with a merry heart.	Eccl 9:7

God's Word Is Health

Health (Medicine) words to live by:
Prov 3:8   Health to thy navel (KJV)
Prov 4:22   Health to all thy flesh (KJV)
Prov 16:24 Pleasant words are health to the bones (KJV)
Prov 12:18 Tongue of the wise brings healing (AMP)
Prov 17:22 A merry heart doeth good as a medicine (KJV)

Merry means goodness, beauty, excellence, cheerfulness, well-being, good things, best things, wealth, health, happiness, prosperity, fairness, graciousness (Strong's Concordance)

Ways to develop a merry heart and a cheerful countenance include avoiding hindrance to your prayer life by practicing forgiveness, controlling your tongue, transforming your thoughts with the Word of God, meditating on God's Word, and surrounding yourself with people of like faith and interests.

Chapter 8
Preparation for the Unexpected

Meditation on God's Word will keep us focused on the necessity of staying in the Holy Spirit and will remind us to include Him in our daily lifestyle. He will forewarn and prepare us for the possible and potential experiences that we may encounter. He will confirm information that we already know, expand our revelation knowledge, show us things to come, pray through us as well as be our Strengthener, Helper, Comforter and Counselor. We can learn lessons from the way The American Red Cross and others who have perfected emergency management. Their plans include:

- A well-developed emergency communication plan
- A predetermined meeting place at all times. Knowing the location of your shelter and safe place will save money, time, and lives.
- Always have essentials on hand for you and your family for safety, security and comfort, such as a supply of water, food, extra long-sleeve and long-leg clothing, battery-powered radio and flashlights, extra batteries, whistle, and a state map.
- Keep your prepared disaster kit available and in an easily transportable kit.
- Include special-needs items for you and your family relevant to spiritual growth.

- Keep your insurance policies and a copy of your will in a safe place. Keep photo identification on you (spiritually this means keep Christ-like character and conduct).
- Check on and know the emergency plans of significant others and locations.
- Know escape routes.
- Follow directions explicitly whether to evacuate or shelter in place

If the unexpected is pending or does occur, do the following:

- Follow your plan.
- Do not park or get stuck in your past.
- Trust God.
- Speak God's Word to dispatch and deploy the angels.
- Be directed by the Holy Spirit.
- Stay in your safe place and refuge.
- Apply the spiritual laws of agreeing, binding, and loosing.
- Be quick to forgive self and others.
- Stay under the applied blood of Jesus Christ.
- Decree and pray God's promises in Jesus Christ's Name and authority
- Make demands in the authority and power of Jesus Christ's Name.
- Keep on your shield of faith
- Know, decree, confess and act on Scriptures that God has spoken in the Bible concerning His thoughts that address your experience.
- Align your expectations of the outcome based on what God has said and not on what you are experiencing at that moment.
- Think and act like the victor and not the victim.
- Don't be distracted.
- Having done all you know to do—*Stand*.
- Stay informed.
- Be vigilant and unwavering. Behold, God is my salvation; I will trust, and not be afraid: for the   LORD JEHOVAH *is*

my strength and *my* song; he also is become my salvation. (Isaiah 12:2 KJV)
- Know when to move out and move on and when to stay put.
- Know where, when, and how to use escape route(s).
- Stay in a thanksgiving and praise mode, consistently giving God glory.
- Keep God's Word in your heart and in your mouth.

Chapter 9

Confirming the Plans through Praise and Worship

God inhabits the praises of His people, and as children of Our Most High God we should be dedicated and loyal in our personal praise and worship. This will help us to strengthen our relationship with God, increase our trust in him, and educate us on how to recognize and without hesitation obey His Voice.

The English word *worship* comes from the Old English word *worth-ship*, a word which denotes the worthiness of the one receiving the special honor or devotion. Worship is not an emotional exercise with God, and it is not words that induce certain feelings. Worship is a response built upon truth. If we are to worship in truth, and the Word of God is truth, we must worship out of an understanding of the Word of God.

Our praise is an act of worship or acknowledgment by which the virtues or deeds of God are recognized and extolled. The praise of man toward God is the means by which we express our joy to the Lord. We are to praise God both for who He is and for what He does (Psalm 150:2). Praising God for who He is called *adoration*; praising Him for what he does is known as *thanksgiving*. Praise of God may be in song or prayer, individually or collectively, spontaneous or prearranged, and originating from the emotions or from the will. The Godly person will echo David's words, "My praise shall be continually of You ... And [I] will praise You yet more and more" (Psalm 71:6, 14).

The following chart gives an overview of the practice and power of praise:

Illustration 4 – Practice and Power of Praise

The following chart gives an overview of the practice and power of praise:

WORD	SCRIPTURE	MEANING
Laudation A Hymn (Strong's #1867)	Ps 22:3 Rom 15:11	God inhabits the praises of his people. Praise with your applause
Strength in various applications (*force, security, majesty, praise*)—boldness, loud, might, power, strength, strong. (Strong's #5797)	Ps 8:2	Praise silences the enemy and avenger.
Properly an *extension* of the hand, that is, (by implication) *avowal,* or (usually) *adoration;* specifically a *choir* of worshippers:—confession, (sacrifice of) praise, thanks (giving, offering).	Ps 50:14-15 Ps 107:22	Praise brings deliverance. I will offer to God the sacrifice of thanksgiving and pay my vows to the LORD. And let them sacrifice the sacrifices of thanksgiving, and declare his works with rejoicing
Exultation; specifically *welcome*—gladness, (exceeding) joy.	Acts 2:47	Praise causes magnification and favor with all people.
A *praising* (the act), that is, (specifically) a *thank* (offering)—praise.	Heb 13:15; Ps 34:1	Praise is an attitude of my heart. I offer the sacrifice of praise continually to my God.
Magnify—to lift up; to extol with praise	Ps 34:3; Ps 69:30	O magnify the Lord with me and let us exalt His Name together. I will praise the name of God with a song, and will magnify him with thanksgiving.
Yadah (Strong's #3034)	2 Chron 20; Ps 134:2; Ps 141:2; 1 Kg 8:22; 1 Tim 2:8	Throw up hands in total dependence on God.
Towdah (Strong's #8426)	Ps 50:23—Whoso offereth praise glorifieth me: and to him that ordereth *his* conversation *aright* will I show the salvation of God.	Praise glorifies God and results in salvation, defined as deliverance, safety, preservation, healing, soundness, pardon, and wholeness. Used for thanking

Illustration 4 – Practice and Power of Praise

WORD	SCRIPTURE	MEANING
	conversation *aright* will I show the salvation of God.	soundness, pardon, and wholeness. Used for thanking God for "things not yet received" as well as things already at hand. It means to show agreement with by extending the right hand. Be thankful.
Sabach (Strong's #7623)	Ps 145; 47; 100	To make a loud noise. To commend, to triumph, to exclaim, glory, shout"
Zamar (Strong's # 2167)	Ps 149:3, 144; 150; Rom. 12:1; Eph 5:19-20	Use body as a musical instrument to praise God Singing songs put to music.
Alleluia	Rev 19:1, 3-4, 6	A primary Hebrew word for praise. Our word *hallelujah* comes from this base. Applaud and give God a praise offering for who He is. An adoring exclamation!
Tehillah (Strong's #8416)	(Ps 22:3)—But thou *art* holy, *O thou* that inhabitest the praises of Israel.	Simply means, "to sing, to laud." "God is enthroned on the praises (tehillah) of Israel." This is the kind of praise that God dwells in. Any form of singing can be praise, but one of the higher forms was the Dorean mode which was in neither the western major nor oriental minor keys. It was sort of chanting whereby the words of Halal were melodiously chanted. This is the expression of praise the Psalmist said God inhabited.
Halal (Strong's #1984)	Psalm 148:13-14; 146; 105; 106	It means, "to be clear, to shine, to boast, show, to rave, to celebrate, to be clamorously foolish."

There is no higher law than the law of praise and worship. The appropriate response to receiving what you prayerfully ask for and speak over your circumstance is praise (Hebrews 11:6; Mark 11:24). *Prayer asks, but praise obtains*. It's a faith walk—see Romans 1:17

and 1 Timothy 6:12. Whenever we pray the promises of God as His covenant children, we should believe in, rely on, and trust Him to respond according to the promise that He made and we prayed. So we receive the answer by faith and demonstrate this by praising God *before* ending the prayer. Jesus said:

"Therefore I say unto you, What things soever ye desire, when ye pray, believe that ye receive them, and ye shall have them" (Mark 11:24).

After your prayer, continue to thank and praise God as you patiently wait for full manifestation of the answer. Remember to let patience have her perfect work, being entire and wanting nothing. As you thank and praise God, continue to confess the Scripture(s) that you prayed about your specific circumstance. Don't neglect God's law of agreement. God's Words (Promises) prayed in Jesus Christ's name must be the same ones that you speak over and to your specific circumstance(s). "The just shall live by faith" (Romans 1:17).

It's through our faith walk, prayer time, meditation of Scripture, and praise and worship of God that we remain in an intimate relationship with Jesus Christ. It is through this intimacy and open communication with the Holy Spirit that we receive clarity about God's plans for us and our lives.

> For I know the thoughts I that think toward you, saith the Lord, thoughts of peace, and not of evil to, give you an expected end" (Jeremiah 29:11; KJV).

> "Let the Lord be magnified, which hath pleasure in the prosperity of his servant" (Psalm 35:27; KJV).

Jeremiah and David are reminding us through these two Scriptures that we as children of the Most High God should expect to be blessed with good, prosperity, and salvation (deliverance, help, safety, victory, saving grace of God and God Himself as the author of salvation). What have you been expecting from God? What or who influenced you to this point? What do you enjoy doing and can do well with less effort or frustration than others? Are you a spiritual baby, child, adolescent, or mature Christian? Do you know and are you completely satisfied that God fearfully and wonderfully made you as uniquely you? Do you know and are you demonstrating your spiritual gifts? What are they? Are you demonstrating them to glorify God, and

> For the perfecting of the saints, for the work of the ministry, for the edifying of the body of Christ: Till we all come in the unity of the faith, and of the knowledge of the Son of God, unto a perfect man, unto the measure of the stature of the fullness of Christ:" That we henceforth be no more children, tossed to and fro, and carried about with every wind of doctrine, by the sleight of men, and cunning craftiness, whereby they lie in wait to deceive; But speaking the truth in love, may grow up into him in all things, which is the head, even Christ (Ephesians 4:12-15).

Knowing and appreciating that our spiritual gifts, talents, abilities, treasures (e.g., those things that add value), and Godly relationships are blessings from God keeps us focused. God did not have to wonder and ponder about direction and or victory for us after we were born. He does not have to think up the platform or season of our next assignment, how to keep or get us out of trouble, how to take care of us, or how to always cause us to triumph in Christ Jesus. He purposed what we would be and what we would do before conception.

> Oh yes, you shaped me first inside, then out; you formed me in my mother's womb. I thank you, High God—you're breathtaking! Body and soul, I am marvelously made! I worship in adoration—what a creation!

> You know me inside and out, you know every bone in my body; You know exactly how I was made, bit by bit, how I was sculpted from nothing into something.

> Like an open book, you watched me grow from conception to birth; all the stages of my life were spread out before you, The days of my life all prepared before I'd even lived one day" (Psalm 139:15-16; The Message Bible).

Meditate on this and get it settled that you were born for a specific purpose and you have been programmed and equipped to fulfill that purpose. Resources, potentials, people, and opportunities await you or just have to be developed from within. So let's start this course and employ principles that Jesus taught us. Christ was emphatic about educating His disciples on how to enjoy the trip to heaven in spite of adverse circumstances. Disciples are students who listen, learn, and apply the lessons taught by the teacher for the purpose of changing their behavior to become like the teacher. Christ as the living Word of God, defeated Satan, death, hell, and the grave so that we could live in the victory that He purchased for us as our Redeemer. If you are not currently enjoying the more abundant life, it's not impossible or too late to do so. It begins with your decision to make that commitment.

Chapter 10

Is Your Transportation Reliable?

The body that God made for us is the mode of transportation for our spirits. After reaching the age of accountability (knowing right from wrong), God holds us responsible for applying what we know. Upon being introduced to and learning about Jesus Christ, one must make a decision to accept Him as Lord and Savior in order to know and fulfill God's purpose for their life. Not to accept Him is to reject Him. Being born again of the spirit is the humble beginning of getting to know Christ. According to Romans 10:8-11

> But what saith it? The word is nigh thee, even in thy mouth, and in thy heart: that is, the word of faith, which we preach;
>
> That if thou shalt confess with thy mouth the Lord Jesus, and shalt believe in thine heart that God hath raised him from the dead, thou shalt be saved.
>
> For with the heart man believeth unto righteousness; and with the mouth confession is made unto salvation For the scripture saith, Whosoever believeth on him shall not be ashamed" (KJV).

According to God's plan, it is easy to become born again, get delivered, and have access to the blessings made available to us because of Jesus fulfilling His purpose while He was in the earth. He demonstrated the effectiveness and efficiency of God's Word in all circumstances. He also revealed the importance of speaking God's Word in prayer and over our circumstances. He made it clear that the authority of God's Word was able to create, control, and change the environment. He also demonstrated that God's Word, and not the individual, was the performer of the power that God released into His Word when He first spoke that Word. Thus, every believer has the potential to speak the Word of God and that spoken Word will perform according to the authority and ability that God put in it when He first spoke it. The believing, Word-speaking child of God will never be ashamed (embarrassed or disappointed). So upon reading and meditating on the Word of God, get it in your heart in abundance and speak that same Word out of your mouth only after you believe it. Then, expect to receive the blessings (harvest) from the Word (seed) spoken. Salvation (being born again, delivered, healed, made whole and sound, and safe, preserved and protected) always come by hearing, believing, and confessing the sincere, pure, undefiled, holy Word of God. Then the Word of God does the work by performing the perfect will of God, because God has already decreed that His Word will not return to Him without results. It will accomplish whatever God wants and achieve whatever He (or one of His believing children) sends it to do. All believers should know this and live as though they do.

Once we are born again, our transportation is very reliable because when we accept Jesus Christ as Lord and Savior, the Holy Spirit baptizes each of us into the Body of Christ based on God's specific purpose for that individual's life. Our physical body is the only way that we have to contact this world and is necessary only while we are in the earth. In order to develop a relationship with Jesus Christ, we must develop our spirit man because God's Word is Spirit and Truth. Also God is a Spirit and they that worship Him must do so in Spirit and Truth (His Word). We should feed our spirit the Word of God just as we feed the physical body its food so that our spirits will have strength and authority over our flesh.

How Often to Stop for Fuel

Prayer is communicating with God and is the source of fuel for the soul. It ignites, stimulates, invigorates, encourages, promotes, and stirs up the soul of the believer who knows how to listen as well as talk to God. The soul includes our mind, will, emotions, and intellect. It is the soul of man that Satan attacks. He penetrates our thoughts, infiltrates our minds, and captivates our wills for his ultimate goal of dominating our lives by influencing our decisions. Satan cannot *make* us do anything, and he cannot read our minds. The only way that he knows what we are thinking is by the words spoken through our mouths. The only way that Satan knows if his thoughts are being considered or entertained is when the words that are spoken or sung are the same as the thoughts that he injects into our minds. So, we must evaluate all thoughts before speaking them. If those thoughts do not agree with the Word of God, then they should be cast down and replaced with God's Word. It is very important that we listen for, listen to, and immediately obey the voice of The Holy Spirit. This is done through spending quality time to develop intimacy with the Holy Spirit, prayerfully reading and meditating on the Scriptures. Intimacy cannot be developed through another person. A third person or other people can be involved in introductions; but never in developing intimacy.

Benefits from Reading and Meditating on God's Word

Through prayerful reading and meditating on God's Word we can:

- Get directions on how to make quality decisions
- Receive peace of mind
- Gain courage and confidence
- Roll our cares on the Lord
- Become anxiety free
- Get focused on God's priorities and agendas
- Develop an intimate relationship with God
- Strengthen our spirit's ability to recognize the voice of God at all times

- Grow in the spirit of discernment
- Accept God's forgiveness, forgive ourselves, and forgive others
- Receive clarity of God's purposes and plans
- Enjoy being in the presence of our Heavenly Father
- Increase our faith by hearing God's Word with our spirit
- Receive revelation knowledge
- Continue to develop and demonstrate a thankful, praising, and prayerful attitude
- Learn how to become proficient at quenching all the fiery darts of the enemy
- Become a confidante of God by the Holy Spirit
- Yield to the Holy Spirit as He prays through us
- Receive the complete manifestation of healing
- Always triumph in Christ Jesus and consistently live victoriously

When Christ was in the earth realm, He prayed often and taught His disciples that men should always pray. Christ prayed early in the mornings and at different times during the day. He prayed before, during, and after miracles and other challenges. He prayed in gardens, on mountainsides, on land, on the sea, in the temple, in homes, and in boats. He was and is the Word of God, so while here He spoke to trees, seas, death, sickness, the wind, the devil, and all types of people. We are to follow Christ's example because He is the author and developer of our faith. Keep your eyes on *Jesus,* who both began and finished this race we're in. Study how he did it. Because he never lost sight of where he was headed—that exhilarating finish in and with God—he could put up with anything along the way: the Cross, the shame, whatever. And now he's *there,* in the place of honor, right alongside God. When you find yourself flagging in your faith; go over that story again, item by item—that long litany of hostility he plowed through. *That* will shoot adrenaline into your souls! (Hebrews 12:1-3; Message Bible). When we consider Jesus' approach to difficult people and challenging experiences, we should observe and analyze every part of His life, including His conduct and courage in suffering. It's through Jesus' teachings that we learn how to apply these lessons in longsuffering when dealing with controversial people and patience in addressing difficult things or circumstances. Longsuffering and patience are both associated with the patient quality that will not surrender or succumb when tested or on trial. Practicing what we learn from Jesus, we will not take on a victim mentality but always demonstrate a victor's winning attitude.

Maintenance Check-up

There is a need for a maintenance check-up routinely as outlined in the owner's manual and especially before a long trip. The check-up while journeying on life's highway involves a visit to a mechanic who has special skills and a good reputation. These mechanics may include doctors, nurses, therapists, teachers, parents, mentors, Godly friends, pastors, and others who help to develop and keep us in shape mentally, emotionally, intellectually, spiritually, and physically.

Check Oil and Lubricant—Love Walk

Below are the Greek words and definitions for four types of love

- Agape—selfless love. means "love" (unconditional God-kind of love)
- Phileo-love for friends, means friendship or affectionate love in modern Greek. It is a dispassionate virtuous love, a concept developed by *Aristotle*. it includes loyalty to friends, family, and community, and requires virtue, equality and familiarity
- Eros-erotic love, passionate love, with sensual desire and longing. The Modern Greek word *"erotas"* means "intimate love;" however, *eros* does not have to be sexual in nature.
- Storge—family love. It is natural affection, like that felt by parents for offspring. Rarely used in ancient works and then almost exclusively as a descriptor of relationships within the family.

The goal of all Christians should be to consistently live according to 1 Corinthians 13

1 Corinthians 13 The Way of Love

Though I speak with the tongues of men and of angels, but have not love, I have become sounding brass or a clanging cymbal.

And though I have the gift of prophecy, and understand all mysteries and all knowledge, and though I have all faith, so that I could remove mountains, but have not love, I am nothing.

And though I bestow all my goods to feed the poor, and though I give my body to be burned, but have not love, it profits me nothing.

Love suffers long and is kind; love does not envy; love does not parade itself, is not puffed up; does not behave rudely, does not seek its own, is not provoked, thinks no evil; does not rejoice in iniquity, but rejoices in the truth; bears all things, believes all things, hopes all things, endures all things.

Love never fails. But whether there are prophecies, they will fail; whether there are tongues, they will cease; whether there is knowledge, it will vanish away.

For we know in part and we prophesy in part.

But when that which is perfect has come, then that which is in part will be done away.

When I was a child, I spoke as a child, I understood as a child, I thought as a child; but when I became a man, I put away childish things.

> For now we see in a mirror, dimly, but then face to face. Now I know in part, but then I shall know just as I also am known.
>
> And now abide faith, hope, love, these three; but the greatest of these is love." (KJV)

Faith will not work without love, and we have no hope of success or victory if our faith is not working. Faith without works is dead. Love is the oil and lubricant that keeps us in a forgiving spirit and minimizes the probability of giving any place to the devil such as anger, confusion, envy, strife, or fear. It keeps our focus on demonstrating the character and nature of Christ in all aspects of our lifestyle. To ensure a Christ-like attitude, let's follow the precepts and examples He demonstrated during His victorious and enjoyable journey on earth while en route back to Heaven.

In all of His experiences, whether pleasant or unpleasant, Christ was consistent and disciplined in the way that he dealt with problems, people, and opportunities. He identified opportunities to improve the lives of others by teaching how the Word of God is effective and efficient in dealing with all problems, challenges, and circumstances in life. His strategy included the following:

- An acute and sensitive awareness of the people and all aspects of their culture.
- A respect for each culture, adapting His teachings and examples in a way to be understood by each one.
- A communication style that could reach all ethnicities, ages, intellects, communities, diversities, and similarities to learn obedience.
- To continue to listen to and keep people talking about controversial topics until He heard a truth that He could agree with. He would acknowledge that truth to them and take charge of the conversation by using the Word of God to challenge and clarify areas that they disagreed on. Then, with further sound biblical teaching; He motivated all listeners to desire a transformation in their thinking and a shift in paradigm.

- He explained what causes a person to err. To err means to waiver, wander; be led and/or lead others astray; a mistake; an unconscious or unwitting sin; a fault committed through adversity, hardship, difficulty, danger, misfortune, harsh conditions, or hard times. Erring is different from the presumptuous sin of willfully walking away from God's commandments. Erring is to commit wrong or a fault committed inadvertently in ease or negligence of mind because of rashness or ignorance, but not willfully, being deceived. Let's study how Christ defined error.

> The Sadducees, a religious group who did not believe in the resurrection, asked Christ about the resurrection and marriage. They came to Him saying Teacher, Moses said, if a man die having no children, his brother shall marry his wife, and raise up seed unto his brother. Here's a case where there were seven brothers. The first brother married and died, leaving no child, and his wife passed to his brother. The second brother also left her childless, then the third—and on and on, all seven. Eventually the wife died. Now here's our question: At the resurrection, whose wife is she? She was a wife to each of them" (Matt 22:22-28 The Message Bible).

Christ said that you do err, not knowing the scriptures, nor the power of God. (Matt 22:29 KJV). Then Christ explains to them that the purpose of marriage is to replenish the earth and keep the race going. Resurrected saints and angels do not die and do not need to marry to keep their kind in existence.

The Sadducees studied and quoted the books of Moses as though Moses' sayings were their only source of confidence concerning the laws and Word of God. So Jesus quoted to them God's Word from their source of confidence.

> But as touching the resurrection of the dead, have ye not read that which was spoken unto you by God,

saying, I am the God of Abraham, and the God of Isaac, and the God of Jacob? God is not the God of the dead, but of the living (Matthew 22:31-32; Exodus 3:6, 16).

Christ taught them that God is not the God of dead bodies but of immortal souls. In that setting all who heard Jesus were astonished and in awe of His teachings. Let us always be reminded that when we transition from this life, our souls will never die but will live together in one of two places. Our eternal resting place is determined by our acceptance or rejection of Jesus Christ in this life. Avoid being self-deceived. Chapter 11 lists the reasons that one may err. This list will serve as a maintenance checklist for you. Be encouraged to study your manufacturer's manual (The Bible) to correct the problem.

Chapter 11
Reasons People Err

- Not knowing the Scriptures or the power of God (ignorance and/or a lack of knowledge of what God has said and His authority and ability to do anything (Matthew 22:29; KJV)
- Being proud and arrogant causes one to wander away from God's commandments resulting in error and rebuke or being accursed (Psalm 119:21)
- They which lead thee caused thee to err and destroy the way of thy paths (Isaiah 3:12; KJV).
- Following those who do not know the Scriptures or the power of God leads to captivity, a victim mentality, and being at the mercy of your circumstances and environment (Isaiah 5:13).
- People so err in their hearts and have not known the ways of the LORD (Psalm 95:10 KJV).
- Error can be caused through wine and strong drink; they err in vision, they stumble in judgment (Isaiah 28:7)
- A cowardly attitude or soldier who throws down or fails to use their weapon (the Word of God) and flee from battle. Your faith is your shield; so keep it and use it (Ephesians 6:10-18; Hebrews 10:32-39; Habakkuk 2:4). Nehemiah 8:10 tells us that the joy of the Lord is our strength. And I Timothy 6:12 encourages us to fight the good fight of faith **Remember**: Restoration was undertaken by the Messiah through His

intervention and intercession. Compare Isaiah 59:16-17 with Ephesians 6:10-18.
- Love of and coveting after money will lead to erring from the faith (I Timothy 6:9-10).
- Participating in profane, vain babblings and oppositions of science . . . causing erring concerning the faith (1 Timothy 6:20-21; KJV)
    o Profane—To treat anything holy with disrespect. In the Bible, many things could be profaned by disregarding God's laws about their correct use: the Sabbath (Isaiah 56:6), the Temple (Acts 24:6), the covenant (Mal 2:10), and God's name (Lev 18:21) The term *profane* is often applied to foolish or irresponsible people. Esau, who sold his birthright, was a "profane" person (Hebrews 12:16).
    o Vain babblings—empty, worthlessness, or futile/ineffective/useless, void, nonproductive. Lacks satisfying man's need for salvation and the molding of the Christian life and character. Void of any divine or spiritual character.

The Remedy for When Error Occurs:

- Repent, confess, receive forgiveness, and forgive yourself
- Be not rash with your mouth.
- Let your heart not be hasty to utter vows before the God
- When you make a vow to God be sure that you pay it.
- Suffer not your mouth to cause your flesh to sin.
- Do not say to the recording angel that your sin was only an error.
- Do not marvel/be in awe at seeing the oppression of the poor.
- Do not marvel at the perversion, distortion, falsification, or twisting of justice.
- Study, meditate on, and apply the Word of God in all your decision making.
- Always abide in Jesus.
- Pray without ceasing.
- Rejoice in the Lord always.
- Become and stay equally yoked with believers.

- Be led by the Holy Spirit.
- Confess only those words that you want a harvest from; Confession brings possession. You have what you continue to say.
- Don't let anyone define you by their opinions.
- Remember the law of seedtime and harvest. Before a harvest, there must be seed (God's Word planted in an open, receptive, heart).
- Refrain from lust, covetousness, and the love of money.
- Have no idol gods.
- Follow after righteousness, godliness, faith, love, patience, and meekness.
- Fight the good fight of faith. Don't allow anything or anybody to keep you from developing your faith.
- Lay hold of eternal life, whereunto thou art also called, and hast professed a good profession before many witnesses.

Being Transformed by the Renewing of Your Mind

We have been instructed to lay hold of eternal life whereunto we are also called. God calls to embrace, employ, educate, and empower His children for work in His vineyard. It is a divine invitation to participate in the blessings of redemption. It suggests either vocation or destination. So, God calls us to do, go, or be. The idea of transformation refers to an invisible process in Christians, which takes place or begins and continues to take place during our life in this age. As we study and meditate the Word of God, our thoughts and images are to be the same as His were when He first spoke that Word. Renewing of our minds by transformation is similar to the process that occurs during the metamorphosis process of the caterpillar to the butterfly. A renewed mind in Christ is physically manifested by a completely different form or appearance. The change is different in nature and form. This includes a change in interest, desire, image, confidence, courage, soaring capacity, and response to the environment, motivation, attitude, acquaintance, and knowledge of God, application of God's Word and development of potential. God's Word has creative ability and power for us and in us. Christ told our Heavenly Father in

John 17:16 that we as members of His body (e.g., the church) are not defined by the world nor are we marked by this world's boundaries. We have unlimited potential and the only limits are self imposed.

Successful Arrival to Our Destination

God has decreed that His Word always performs what He purposed and empowered it to do. It is God's Word that does the performing through the believer. God empowered then spoke His Word with every intention of performing every jot and tittle of it. So as we are transformed into the image of Christ, the same power that God put in His Word when He first spoke it is released into our circumstances when we believe and speak the same thing that God spoke. It is not by power, nor by might, but by the Spirit of God that overshadows and releases the power of God's Word in any situation or circumstance that we want to create, control, or change. The mind of Christ in us creates images in us that influence our thoughts, words, and actions. As we journey through life, viewing it as Christ did in His earthly walk, we will keep the course as we fulfill our destiny through all seasons in all types of weather. We will be victorious over the storms of life and not be overcome or overwhelmed by any of the challenges. When we complete our earthly assignment and have deposited into the earth all the gifts, talents, skills and blessings that God entrusted to us, we will arrive at our final destination having enjoyed every step of the journey. Abundance and rewards awaits us as we hear these words:

"Well done *thou* good and faithful servant, thou has been *faithful* over a few things, I will make thee ruler over many things; enter into the joy of thy lord" (Matt 25:21)

Bibliography

Bible Study Tools. (n.d.). Retrieved July 2014, from Easton Bible Study Tools: http://www.biblestudytools.com/dictionaries/eastons-bible-dictionary/

Brody, J. E. (1988, April 7). *HEALTH; Personal Health*. Retrieved July 2014, from The New York Times: http://www.nytimes.com/1988/04/07/us/health-personal-health.html?module=-Search&mabReward=relbias%3Aw%2C%7B%222%22%3A%22RI%3A14%22%7D

Carbonell, M. (2006). *Discover Your Giftedness: Discover Your Divine Design...the Unique You.* Barnesville, Georgia, USA: Christian Impact Ministries.

Carlson, R. (1972). *You Can Be Happy, No Matter What.* Novato: New World Library.

Collier, J. (2011). *Living inthe Faith Dimensions.* Kansas City: Walker Five Publications.

Covey, S. (1989). The 7 Habits of Highly Effective People. New York: Fireside.

Fairchild, M. (n.d.). *The Healing Power of Laughter.* Retrieved July 2014, from About.com Christianity: http://christianity.about.

com/od/topicaldevotions/qt/laughtertherapy.htm

Family Education Staff. (2014). *Normal Adolescent Development.* Retrieved July 2014, from Family Education: http://life.familyeducation.com/puberty/growth-and-development/36357.html?page=2&detoured=1

Farlex Inc. (n.d.). *The Free Dictionary.* Retrieved July 2014, from The Free Dictionary: http://www.thefreedictionary.com/

Hagin, K. (1979). *Growing up Spiritually.* USA: Faith Library.

Jolly, W. (1999). *A Setback Is a Setup for a Comeback.* New York: St. Martin's Press.

Laughter is Good Medicine. (1989, January 31). *Birmingham News–Health/Science Section* .

Laughter is the Best Medicine for Your Heart. (2009, July 14). Retrieved July 2014, from University of Maryland Medical Center: http://www.umm.edu/news-and-events/news-release/2009/laughter-is-the-best-medicine-for-your-heart

Laughter Yoga: Health and Fitness Craze Sweeping the World. (n.d.). Retrieved July 2014, from Laughter Yoga University: http://www.laughteryoga.org/english/home

Lawrence Robinson & Jeanne Segal, P. (2014, Updated July). *Help for Parents of Troubled Teens: Dealing with Anger, Violence, Dilenquency and other Teen Behavior Problems.* Retrieved July 2014, from Help Guide: http://www.helpguide.org/mental/troubled-teens.htm

Lillas, C. &. (2009). Infant/Child Mental Health, Early Intervention, and Relationship-Based Therapies: A Neurorelational Framework for Interdisciplinary Practice. New York : W.W. Norton.

Ljungdahl, L. (1989, January 27). *Laugh If This is a Joke*. Retrieved July 2014, from JAMA: The Journal of the American Medical Association: http://jama.jamanetwork.com/journal.aspx

Munroe, M. (1996). Maximizing Your Potential: The Keys to Dying Empty. Phildelphia: Destiny Image.

New Study Proves that Laughter Really is the Best Medicine. (2014, April 22). Retrieved July 2014, from Huffington Post: http://www.huffingtonpost.com/2014/04/22/laughter-and-memory n 5192086.html

New Years Resolution Stastics. (2014, 1). Retrieved July 2014, from Statistic Brain: http://www.statisticbrain.com

Norman Cousins. (2014, March 26). Retrieved July 2014, from Wikipedia: http://en.wikipedia.org/wiki/Norman Cousins

O'Neal, W. (2012). *The Young Man and the Mentor.* Maitland: Zulon Press.

Strong, J. (1990). The New Strong's Exhaustive Concordance of The Bible. Nashville: Thomas Nelson.

Swindoll, C. (1983). *Growing Strong in the Season's of Life.* Portland: Multnomah Press.

Thomas, S. &. (1986, June). Costing Nursing Service Using RVUs. *Journal of Nursing Administration Vol 16 No 12* , pp. 10-16.

Vines, W. Child, Blasphemy, Evil Speaking, Foolish, Ignorance. In W. Vines, *Vines Dictionary of New Testament Words (Unabridged Edition)* (pp. 134, 190, 392, 454, 585). McLean: McDonald.

Walton, O. (n.d.). *Greek and Hebrew Words for Praise.* Retrieved July 2014, from Exceeding Faith Ministries: www.exceedingfaith.com

Where are the 7 Ways to Worship God in the Bible? (n.d.). Retrieved July 2014, from The Bible Alive: http://biblealive.us/

Wilson, W. Joy, Laughter, Merry. In W. Wilson, *Wilson's Old Testament Word Studies (Unadbridged Edition)* (pp. 234,244,274). McClean: McDonald.

Worship–Definition. (n.d.). Retrieved July 2014, from Wikipedia: http://en.wikipedia.org/wiki/Worship

Your New Year's Resolution Online Poll Results Are In! (2012, February 3). Retrieved July 2014, from Snap Surveys: http://www.snapsurveys.com/blog/new-years-resolution-online-poll-results

About the Author

Surpora Sparks-Thomas, MBA, BSN, RN, FAAN is Chief Nurse Executive Emeritus of Children's of Alabama. Her nursing career spans 50 years with experience as a staff nurse and successive supervisory experience working every nursing level for 20 years and subsequent 28 years as the Chief Nurse Executive/Sr. VP Nursing of the then Children's Health System; retiring January 1, 2010. Mrs. Thomas has been inducted into the Alabama Health Care Hall of Fame, the Alabama Nursing Hall of Fame, the Pediatric Nursing Hall of Fame, International Sigma Theta Tau Nursing Honor Society and as a Fellow in The American Academy of Nursing. In November 2001, The Children's Hospital Board of Trustees and Executive Administrative Staff named and dedicated The Surpora Thomas Pediatric Nursing Education & Research Center in her honor. The Surpora Thomas Nursing Excellence Fund to support Nursing Research was established in December 2009. One of the hallmarks of her visionary leadership is the successful application of biblical principles in her strategic planning and decision making processes.

Surpora Sparks-Thomas received her calling and anointing to teach in 1976. Christ specifically instructed her to teach revelation knowledge to others as the Holy Spirit would teach her. Christ also instructed her to teach in a way that the hearers would understand how to skillfully apply the word of God to create their own prosperity and success. Christ promised to give her an abundance of revelations that she must pass on to others. Christ has kept His promise and she has her commitment.

Thomas is an Evangelist who glorifies God and serves others as an anointed bible teacher, Sunday school teacher, Deaconess, and Director of Christian Education at The New Bethlehem Missionary Baptist Church in Dolomite, Alabama. She is also an author and poet who has earned certifications as a Human Behavior Consultant, a Christian Life Coach, and Facilitator for Covey's 7 Habits of Highly Effective People.

She has been blessed with many awards and recognition from community, civic, professional, political and religious groups. Her successes in life serve as infallible proof that timely application of relevant biblical principles always creates success. Evangelist Thomas personal testimony is that declaration and application of biblical principles created success in the corporate world and her personal life. Those who were taught how to and applied the principles as well as those who witnessed their results continue to validate this as true. Others who confirm that the principles outlined in this book are effective include hearers of the hourly weekly bible study class and those who listen to the weekly thirty minute radio broadcast. Evangelist Thomas is an experienced, gifted and anointed keynote speaker for Christian, Corporate, and other secular events, retreats, workshops, seminars, special events, and conferences.

In all endeavors, Surpora continues to enjoy life with Jule, her husband for 51 years of marriage, who is also her best friend, and confidante. Jule and Surpora live in Birmingham, Alabama and are blessed with four daughters (Sonya, Sherri, Julena, and Leah); two son-in-laws (Eric and Tremaine) three granddaughters (Erica, Erin, and Taylor); two grandsons (DeMaris & Jule) and one great grandson (Kamari). They are also blessed with and enjoy a large network of other family members and friends.

Summary

Now that you have completed reading "Equipped *to Enjoy Life's Journey*", get excited and be encouraged to apply what you learned. I am and many others are infallible proof that the principles in this book work every time on time. They will work in any setting, from any forum, for any person who believes decrees and exercises their faith in expecting the desired results. Get going with the business of living out your potential and completing your earthly assignments. Glorify God and empty all that He has entrusted you with in the earth to be blessed and for you to be a blessing. Be encouraged to go, be and do all that God designed and destined you for before you came to earth. Live it with joy!

Get the same image of yourself that God has of you. Let the Word of God create that image for you. You will never perform above the image that you have of yourself.

If you completed the assessment tools you know a lot more about why you behave the way that you do. You have also developed a plan to implement and use to take authority of and dominion over your circumstances. If you have not developed your plan yet, make it a priority to do so. Share with an accountability party to help keep you focused, encouraged, empowered, engaged. and responsible. If you employ the principles that you learned from reading this book, your life will never be the same in Jesus name. I thank God for you and praise Him with you in Jesus name for the revelation knowledge that the Holy Spirit revealed to us through this book. Give Him Glory!

Surpora Sparks-Thomas

Contact the Author
Surpora Sparks-Thomas
P.O. Box 110463
Birmingham, Al 35211
website: www.surporasparksthomas.com

www.ingramcontent.com/pod-product-compliance
Ingram Content Group UK Ltd.
Pitfield, Milton Keynes, MK11 3LW, UK
UKHW022223230426
12048UKWH00016BA/1027